CW00765811

U 1

SRI AUROBINDO AND THE MOTHER

ON

EDUCATION

SRI AUROBINDO ASHRAM
PONDICHERRY

First edition 1956
Fourteenth impression 2006

Price Rs 45
ISBN-10: 81-7058-028-5
ISBN-13: 978-81-7058-028-7

© Sri Aurobindo Ashram Trust 1956
Published by Sri Aurobindo Ashram Publication Department
Pondicherry - 605 002
Web: http://sabda.sriaurobindoashram.org

Printed at Sri Aurobindo Ashram Press, Pondicherry
PRINTED IN INDIA

CONTENTS

Sri Aurobindo

The Mother

SRI AUROBINDO ON EDUCATION

A Preface on National Education

A Preface on National Education was published in two parts in the last two issues of the *Arya*, Nov.- Dec. 1920 and January 1921. As the journal was discontinued, the series remained incomplete.

A PREFACE ON NATIONAL EDUCATION*

1

The necessity and unmixed good of universal education has become a fixed dogma to the modern intelligence, a thing held to be beyond dispute by any liberal mind or awakened national conscience, and whether the tenet be or not altogether beyond cavil, it may at any rate be presumed that it answers to a present and imperative need of the intellectual and vital effort of the race. But there is not quite so universal an agreement or common attainment to a reasoned or luminous idea on what education is or practically or ideally should be. Add to this uncertainty the demand — naturally insistent and clamorous with the awakening of the spirit of independence in a country like our own which is peculiarly circumstanced not only by the clash of the Asiatic and the European or occidental consciousness and the very different civilisations they have created and the enforced meeting of the English and the Indian mind and culture, but by a political subjection which has left the decisive shaping and supreme control of education in the hands of foreigners, — add the demand for a national type of education, and in the absence of clear ideas on the subject we are likely to enter, as we have in fact entered into an atmosphere of great and disconcerting confusion.

For if we do not know very clearly what education in general truly is or should be, we seem still less to know what we mean by national education. All that appears to be almost unanimously agreed on is that the teaching given in the existing schools and universities has been bad in kind and in addition denationalising, degrading and impoverishing to the national mind, soul and character because it is overshadowed by a foreign hand and foreign in aim, method, substance and spirit. But this purely negative agreement does not carry us very far: it does not tell us what in principle or practice we desire or ought to put in its place. There may be much virtue in an epithet but to tag on the word "national" to a school or college or even a Council or Board of Education, to put that into the hands of an indigenous agency, mostly of men trained in the very system we are denouncing, to reproduce that condemned system with certain differences, additions, subtractions, modifications of detail and curriculum, to tack on a technical side and think we have solved the problem does not really change anything. To be satisfied with a trick of this kind is to perform a somersault round our centre of intellectual gravity, land ourselves where we were before and think we have got into quite another country, — obviously a very unsatisfactory proceeding. The institutions that go by the new name may or may not be giving a better education than the others, but in what they are more national, is not altogether clear even to the most willingly sympathetic critical intelligence.

The problem indeed is one of surpassing difficulty and it is not easy to discover from what point of thought or of practice one has to begin, on what principle to create or on what lines to map out the new building. The conditions are intricate and the thing that is to be created in a way entirely new. We cannot be satisfied with a mere resuscitation of some past principle, method and system that may have happened to prevail at one time in India, however great it was or in consonance with our past civilisation and culture. That reversion would be a sterile and impossible effort hopelessly inadequate to the pressing demands of the present and the far greater demands of our future. On the other hand to take over the English, German or American school and university or some variation on them with a gloss of Indian colour is a course attractively facile and one that saves the need of thinking and of new experiment; but in that case there is no call for this loud pother about nationalising education, all that is needed is a change of control, of the medium of instruction, of the frame and fitting of the curriculum and to some extent of the balance of subjects. I presume that it is something more profound, great and searching that we have in mind and that, whatever the difficulty of giving it shape, it is an education proper to the Indian soul and need and temperament and culture that we are in quest of, not indeed something faithful merely to the past, but to the developing soul of India, to her future need, to the greatness of her coming self-creation, to her eternal spirit. It is this that we have to get clear in our minds and for that we must penetrate down to fundamentals and make those firm before we can greatly execute. Otherwise nothing is easier than to start off on a false but specious cry or from an unsound starting-point and travel far away from the right path on a tangent that will lead us to no goal but only to emptiness and failure.

But first let us clear out of the way or at least put in its proper place and light the preliminary disabling objection that there is and can be no meaning at all or none worth troubling about in the idea of a national education and that the very notion is the undesirable and unprofitable intrusion of a false and narrow patriotism into a field in which patriotism apart from the need of a training in good citizenship has no legitimate place. And for that one purpose no special kind or form of education is needed, since the training to good citizenship must be in all essentials the same whether in the East or the West, England or Germany or Japan or India. Mankind and its needs are the same everywhere and truth and knowledge are one and have no country; education too must be a thing universal and without nationality or borders. What, for an instance, could be meant by a national education in Science, and does it signify that we are to reject modern truth and modern method of science because they come to us from Europe, and go back to the imperfect scientific knowledge of classical India, exile Galileo and Newton and all that came after and teach only what was known to Bhaskara, Aryabhatta and Varahamihira? Or how should the teaching of Sanskrit or the living indigenous tongues differ in kind and method from the teaching of Latin or the living modern tongues in Europe? Are we then to fetch back to the methods of the "Tols" of Nadiya or to the system, if we can find out what it was, practised in ancient Takshashila or Nalanda? At most what can be demanded is a larger place for the study of the past of our country, the replacement of English by the indigenous tongues as a medium and the relegation of the former to the position of a second language, — but it is possible to challenge the advisability even of these changes. After all we live in the twentieth century and cannot revive the India of Chandragupta or Akbar; we must keep abreast with the march of truth and knowledge, fit ourselves for existence under actual circumstances, and our education must be therefore up to date in form and substance and modern in life and spirit.

All these objections are only pertinent if directed against the travesty of the idea of national education which would make of it a means of an obscurantist retrogression to the past forms that were once a living frame of our culture but are now dead or dying things; but that is not the idea nor the endeavour. The living spirit of the demand for national education no more requires a return to the astronomy and mathematics of Bhaskara or the forms of the system of Nalanda than the living spirit of Swadeshi a return from railway and motor traction to the ancient chariot and the bullock-cart. There is no doubt plenty of retrogressive sentimentalism about and there have been some queer violences on common sense and reason and disconcerting freaks that prejudice the real issue, but these inconsequent streaks of fantasy give a false hue to the matter. It is the spirit, the living and vital issue that we have to do with, and there the question is not between modernism and antiquity, but between an imported civilisation and the greater possibilities of the Indian mind and nature, not between the present and the past, but between the present and the future. It is not a return to the fifth century but an initiation of the centuries to come, not a reversion but a break forward away from a present artificial falsity to her own greater innate potentialities that is demanded by the soul, by the Shakti of India.

The argument against national education proceeds in the first place upon the lifeless academic notion that the subject, the acquiring of this or that kind of information is the whole or the central matter. But the acquiring of various kinds of information is only one and not the chief of the means and necessities of education: its central aim is the building of the powers of the human mind and spirit, it is the formation or, as I would prefer to view it, the evoking of knowledge and will and of the power to use knowledge, character, culture, — that at least if no more. And this distinction makes an enormous difference. It is true enough that if all we ask for is the acquisition of the information put at our disposal by science, it may be enough to take over the science of the West whether in an undigested whole or in carefully packed morsels. But the major question is not merely what science we learn, but what we shall do with our science and how too, acquiring the scientific mind and recovering the habit of scientific discovery — I leave aside the possibility of the Indian mentality working freely in its own nature discovering new methods or even giving a new turn to physical science — we shall relate it to other powers of the human mind and scientific knowledge to other knowledge more intimate to other and not less light-giving and power-giving parts of our intelligence and nature. And there the peculiar cast of the Indian mind, its psychological tradition, its ancestral capacity, turn, knowledge bring in cultural elements of a supreme importance. A language, Sanskrit or another, should be acquired by whatever method is most natural, efficient and stimulating to the mind and we need not cling there to any past or present manner of teaching: but the vital question is how we are to learn and make use of Sanskrit and the indigenous languages so as to get to the heart and intimate sense of our own culture and establish a vivid continuity between the still living power of our past and the yet uncreated power of our future, and how we are to learn and use English or any other foreign tongue so as to know helpfully the life, ideas and culture of other countries and establish our right relations with the world around us. This is the aim and principle of a true national education, not, certainly, to ignore modern truth and knowledge, but to take our foundation on our own being, our own mind, our own spirit.

The second ground openly or tacitly taken by the hostile argument is that modern, that is to say, European civilisation is the thing that we have to acquire and fit ourselves for, so only can we live and prosper and it is this that our education must do for us. The idea of national education challenges the sufficiency of this assumption. Europe built up her ancient culture on a foundation largely taken from the East, from Egypt, Chaldea, Phoenicia, India, but turned in a new direction and another life-idea by the native spirit and temperament, mind and social genius of Greece and Rome, lost and then recovered it, in part from the Arabs with fresh borrowings from the near East and from India and more widely by the Renaissance, but then too gave it a new turn and direction proper to the native spirit and temperament, mind and social genius of the Teutonic, and the Latin, the Celtic and Slav races. It is the civilisation so created that has long offered itself as the last and imperative word of the mind of humanity, but the nations of Asia are not bound so to accept it, and will do better, taking over in their turn whatever new knowledge or just ideas Europe has to offer, to assimilate them to their own knowledge and culture, their own native temperament and spirit, mind and social genius and out of that create the civilisation of the future. The scientific, rationalistic, industrial, pseudo-democratic civilisation of the West is now in process of dissolution and it would be a lunatic absurdity for us at this moment to build blindly on that sinking foundation. When the most advanced minds of the occident are beginning to turn in this red evening of the West for the hope of a new and more spiritual civilisation to the genius of Asia, it would be strange if we could think of nothing better than to cast away our own self and potentialities and put our trust in the dissolving and moribund past of Europe.

And, finally, the objection grounds itself on the implicit idea that the mind of man is the same everywhere and can everywhere be passed through the same machine and uniformly constructed to order. That is an old and effete superstition of the reason which it is time now to renounce. For within the universal mind and soul of humanity is the mind and soul of the individual with its infinite variation, its commonness and its uniqueness, and between them there stands an intermediate power, the mind of a nation, the soul of a people. And of all these three education must take account if it is to be, not a machine-made fabric, but a true building or a living evocation of the powers of the mind and spirit of the human being.

<h1 style="text-align:center">2</h1>

These preliminary objections made to the very idea of national education and, incidentally, the misconceptions they oppose once out of the way, we have still to formulate more positively what the idea means to us, the principle and the form that national education must take in India, the thing to be achieved and the method and turn to be given to the endeavour. It is here that the real difficulty begins because we have for a long time, not only in education but in almost all things, in our whole cultural life, lost hold of the national spirit and idea and there has been as yet no effort of clear, sound and deep thinking or seeing which would enable us to recover it and therefore no clear agreement or even clear difference of opinion on essentials and accessories. At the most we have been satisfied with a strong sentiment and a general but shapeless idea and enthusiasm corresponding to the sentiment and have given to it in the form whatever haphazard application chanced to be agreeable to our intellectual associations, habits or caprices. The result has been no tangible or enduring success, but rather a maximum of confusion and failure. The first thing needed is to make clear to our own minds what the national spirit, temperament, idea, need demands of us through education and apply it in its right harmony to all the different elements of the problem. Only after that is done can we really hope with some confidence and chance of utility and success to replace the present false, empty and mechanical education by something better than a poor and futile chaos or a new mechanical falsity, by a real, living and creative upbringing of the Indian manhood of the future.

But first it is necessary to disengage from all ambiguities what we understand by a true education, its essential sense, its fundamental aim and significance. For we can then be sure of our beginnings and proceed securely to fix the just place and whole bearing of the epithet we seek to attach to the word. I must be sure what education itself is or should be before I can be sure what a national education is or should be. Let us begin then with our initial statement, as to which I think there can be no great dispute that there are three things which have to be taken into account in a true and living education, the man, the individual in his commonness and in his uniqueness, the nation or people and universal humanity. It follows that that alone will be a true and living education which helps to bring out to full advantage, makes ready for the full purpose and scope of human life all that is in the in-

dividual man, and which at the same time helps him to enter
into his right relation with the life, mind and soul of the
people to which he belongs and with that great total life,
mind and soul of humanity of which he himself is a unit and
his people or nation a living, a separate and yet inseparable
member. It is by considering the whole question in the light
of this large and entire principle that we can best arrive at a
clear idea of what we would have our education to be and
what we shall strive to accomplish by a national education.
Most is this largeness of view and foundation needed here
and now in India, the whole energy of whose life purpose
must be at this critical turning of her destinies directed to her
one great need, to find and rebuild her true self in individual
and in people and to take again, thus repossessed of her inner
greatness, her due and natural portion and station in the life
of the human race.

There are however very different conceptions possible of
man and his life, of the nation and its life and of humanity
and the life of the human race, and our idea and endeavour
in education may well vary considerably according to that
difference. India has always had her own peculiar conception and vision of these things and we must see whether it is
not really, as it is likely to be, that which will be or ought to
be at the very root of our education and the one thing that
will give it its truly national character. Man has not been
seen by the thought of India as a living body developed
by physical Nature which has evolved certain vital propensities, an ego, a mind and a reason, an animal of the genus
homo and in our case of the species *homo indicus*, whose
whole life and education must be turned towards a satisfaction of these propensities under the government of a trained
mind and reason and for the best advantage of the personal

and the national ego. It has not been either the turn of her mind to regard man pre-eminently as a reasoning animal, or let us say, widening the familiar definition, a thinking, feeling and willing natural existence, a mental son of physical Nature, and his education as a culture of the mental capacities, or to define him as a political, social and economic being and his education as a training that will fit him to be an efficient, productive and well disciplined member of the society and the State. All these are no doubt aspects of the human being and she has given them a considerable prominence subject to her large vision, but they are outward things, parts of the instrumentation of his mind, life and action, not the whole or the real man.

India has seen always in man the individual a soul, a portion of the Divinity enwrapped in mind and body, a conscious manifestation in Nature of the universal self and spirit. Always she has distinguished and cultivated in him a mental, an intellectual, an ethical, dynamic and practical, an aesthetic and hedonistic, a vital and physical being, but all these have been seen as powers of a soul that manifests through them and grows with their growth, and yet they are not all the soul, because at the summit of its ascent it arises to something greater than them all, into a spiritual being, and it is in this that she has found the supreme manifestation of the soul of man and his ultimate divine manhood, his *paramārtha* and highest *puruṣārtha*. And similarly India has not understood by the nation or people an organised State or an armed and efficient community well prepared for the struggle of life and putting all at the service of the national ego, — that is only the disguise of iron armour which masks and encumbers the national Purusha, — but a great communal soul and life that has appeared in the whole and has manifested a nature of its own and a law of that nature, a Swabhava and Swadharma, and embodied it in its intellectual, aesthetic, ethical, dynamic, social and political forms and culture. And equally then our cultural conception of humanity must be in accordance with her ancient vision of the universal manifesting in the human race, evolving through life and mind but with a high ultimate spiritual aim, — it must be the idea of the spirit, the soul of humanity advancing through struggle and concert towards oneness, increasing its experience and maintaining a needed diversity through the varied culture and life motives of its many peoples, searching for perfection through the development of the powers of the individual and his progress towards a diviner being and life, but feeling out too though more slowly after a similar perfectibility in the life of the race. It may be disputed whether this is a true account of the human or the national being, but if it is once admitted as a true description, then it should be clear that the only true education will be that which will be an instrument for this real working of the spirit in the mind and body of the individual and the nation. That is the principle on which we must build, that the central motive and the guiding ideal. It must be an education that for the individual will make its one central object the growth of the soul and its powers and possibilities, for the nation will keep first in view the preservation, strengthening and enrichment of the nation-soul and its Dharma and raise both into powers of the life and ascending mind and soul of humanity. And at no time will it lose sight of man's highest object, the awakening and development of his spiritual being.

A System of National Education
(Some preliminary ideas)

"A System of National Education" was first published in 1921 in an unauthorised edition. The authorised edition was issued in 1924 with the following note:

These essays were first published in the *Karmayogin* in the year 1910. They are, however, incomplete and the subject of national education proper has not been touched except in certain allusions. It was not the author's intention to have them reprinted in their present form, but circumstances have made necessary the bringing out of an authorised edition. The book, as it stands, consists of a number of introductory essays insisting on certain general principles of a sound system of teaching applicable for the most part to national education in any country. As such it may stand as a partial introduction to the subject of national education in India.

I

THE HUMAN MIND

The true basis of education is the study of the human mind, infant, adolescent and adult. Any system of education founded on theories of academic perfection, which ignores the instrument of study, is more likely to hamper and impair intellectual growth than to produce a perfect and perfectly equipped mind. For the educationist has to do, not with dead material like the artist or sculptor, but with an infinitely subtle and sensitive organism. He cannot shape an educational masterpiece out of human wood or stone; he has to work in the elusive substance of mind and respect the limits imposed by the fragile human body.

There can be no doubt that the current educational system of Europe is a great advance on many of the methods of antiquity, but its defects are also palpable. It is based on an insufficient knowledge of human psychology, and it is only safeguarded in Europe from disastrous results by the refusal of the ordinary student to subject himself to the processes it involves, his habit of studying only so much as he must to avoid punishment or to pass an immediate test, his resort to active habits and vigorous physical exercise. In India the disastrous effects of the system on body, mind and character are only too apparent. The first problem in a national system of education is to give an education as comprehensive as the European and more thorough, without the evils of strain and cramming. This can only be done by studying the instruments of knowledge and finding a system of teaching which shall be natural, easy and effective. It is only by strengthening and sharpening these instruments to their utmost capacity that they can be made effective for the increased work which modern conditions require. The muscles of the mind must be thoroughly trained by simple and easy means; then, and not till then, great feats of intellectual strength can be required of them.

The first principle of true teaching is that nothing can be taught. The teacher is not an instructor or task-master, he is a helper and a guide. His business is to suggest and not to impose. He does not actually train the pupil's mind, he only shows him how to perfect his instruments of knowledge and helps and encourages him in the process. He does not impart knowledge to him, he shows him how to acquire knowledge for himself. He does not call forth the knowledge that is within; he only shows him where it lies and how it can be habituated to rise to the surface. The distinction that reserves this principle for the teaching of adolescent and adult minds and denies its application to the child, is a conservative and unintelligent doctrine. Child or man, boy or girl, there is only one sound principle of good teaching. Difference of age only serves to diminish or increase the amount of help and guidance necessary; it does not change its nature.

The second principle is that the mind has to be consulted in its own growth. The idea of hammering the child into the shape desired by the parent or teacher is a barbarous and ignorant superstition. It is he himself who must be induced to expand in accordance with his own nature. There can be no greater error than for the parent to arrange beforehand that his son shall develop particular qualities, capacities, ideas, virtues, or be prepared for a prearranged career. To force the nature to abandon its own *dharma* is to do it permanent harm, mutilate its growth and deface its perfection. It is a selfish tyranny over a human soul and a wound to the nation, which loses the benefit of the best that a man could have given it and is forced to accept instead something imperfect and artificial, second-rate, perfunctory and common. Every one has in him something divine, something his own, a chance of perfection and strength in however small a sphere which God offers him to take or refuse. The task is to find it, develop it and use it. The chief aim of education should be to help the growing soul to draw out that in itself which is best and make it perfect for a noble use.

The third principle of education is to work from the near to the far, from that which is to that which shall be. The basis of a man's nature is almost always, in addition to his soul's past, his heredity, his surroundings, his nationality, his country, the soil from which he draws sustenance, the air which he breathes, the sights, sounds, habits to which he is accustomed. They mould him not the less powerfully because insensibly, and from that then we must begin. We must not take up the nature by the roots from the earth in which it must grow or surround the mind with images and ideas of a life which is alien to that in which it must physically move. If anything has to be brought in from outside, it must be offered, not forced on the mind. A free and natural growth is the condition of genuine development. There are souls which naturally revolt from their surroundings and seem to belong to another age and clime. Let them be free to follow their bent; but the majority languish, become empty, become artificial, if artificially moulded into an alien form. It is God's arrangement that they should belong to a particular nation, age, society, that they should be children of the past, possessors of the present, creators of the future. The past is our foundation, the present our material, the future our aim and summit. Each must have its due and natural place in a national system of education.

II

THE POWERS OF THE MIND

The instrument of the educationist is the mind or *antaḥ-karaṇa*, which consists of four layers. The reservoir of past mental impressions, the *citta* or storehouse of memory, which must be distinguished from the specific act of memory, is the foundation on which all the other layers stand. All experience lies within us as passive or potential memory; active memory selects and takes what it requires from that storehouse. But the active memory is like a man searching among a great mass of locked-up material; sometimes he cannot find what he wants; often in his rapid search he stumbles across many things for which he has no immediate need; often too he blunders and thinks he has found the real thing when it is something else, irrelevant if not valueless, on which he has laid his hand. The passive memory or *citta* needs no training, it is automatic and naturally sufficient to its task; there is not the slightest object of knowledge coming within its field which is not secured, placed and faultlessly preserved in that admirable receptacle. It is the active memory, a higher but less perfectly developed function, which is in need of improvement.

The second layer is the mind proper or *manas*, the sixth sense of our Indian psychology, in which all the others are gathered up. The function of the mind is to receive the images of things translated into sight, sound, smell, taste and touch, the five senses and translate these again into thought-sensations. It receives also images of its own direct grasping and forms them into mental impressions. These sensations and impressions are the material of thought, not thought itself; but it is exceedingly important that thought should work on sufficient and perfect material. It is, therefore, the first business of the educationist to develop in the child the right use of the six senses; to see that they are not stunted or injured by disuse, but trained by the child himself under the teacher's direction to that perfect accuracy and keen subtle sensitiveness of which they are capable. In addition, whatever assistance can be gained by the organs of action, should be thoroughly employed. The hand, for instance, should be trained to reproduce what the eye sees and the mind senses. The speech should be trained to a perfect expression of the knowledge which the whole *antahkarana* possesses.

The third layer is the intellect or *buddhi*, which is the real instrument of thought and that which orders and disposes of the knowledge acquired by the other parts of the machine. For the purpose of the educationist this is infinitely the most important of the three I have named. The intellect is an organ composed of several groups of functions, divisible into two important classes, the functions and faculties of the right-hand, the functions and faculties of the left-hand. The faculties of the right-hand are comprehensive, creative and synthetic; the faculties of the left-hand critical and analytic. To the right-hand belong judgment, imagination, memory, observation; to the left-hand comparison and reasoning. The critical faculties distinguish, compare, classify, generalise, deduce, infer, conclude; they are the component parts of the logical reason. The right-hand faculties comprehend, command, judge in their own right, grasp, hold and manipulate. The right-hand mind is the master of the knowledge, the left-hand its servant. The left-hand touches only the body of knowledge, the right-hand penetrates its soul. The left-hand limits itself to ascertained truth, the right-hand grasps that which is still elusive or unascertained. Both are essential to the completeness of the human reason. These important functions of the machine have all to be raised to their highest and finest working-power, if the education of the child is not to be imperfect and one-sided.

There is a fourth layer of faculty which, not as yet entirely developed in man, is attaining gradually to a wider development and more perfect evolution. The powers peculiar to this highest stratum of knowledge are chiefly known to us from the phenomena of genius, — sovereign discernment, intuitive perception of truth, plenary inspiration of speech, direct vision of knowledge to an extent often amounting to revelation, making a man a prophet of truth. These powers are rare in their higher development, though many possess them imperfectly or by flashes. They are still greatly distrusted by the critical reason of mankind because of the admixture of error, caprice and a biased imagination which obstructs and distorts their perfect workings. Yet it is clear that humanity could not have advanced to its present stage if it had not been for the help of these faculties, and it is a question with which educationists have not yet grappled, what is to be done with this mighty and baffling element, the element of genius in the pupil. The mere instructor does his best to discourage and stifle genius, the more liberal teacher welcomes it. Faculties so important to humanity cannot be left out of our consideration. It is foolish to neglect them. Their imperfect development must be perfected, the admixture of error, caprice and biased fancifulness must be carefully and wisely removed. But the teacher cannot do it; he would eradicate the good corn as well as the tares if he interfered. Here, as in all educational operations, he can only put the growing soul into the way of its own perfection.

III

THE MORAL NATURE

In the economy of man the mental nature rests upon the moral, and the education of the intellect divorced from the perfection of the moral and emotional nature is injurious to human progress. Yet, while it is easy to arrange some kind of curriculum or syllabus which will do well enough for the training of the mind, it has not yet been found possible to provide under modern conditions a suitable moral training for the school and college. The attempt to make boys moral and religious by the teaching of moral and religious text-books is a vanity and a delusion, precisely because the heart is not the mind and to instruct the mind does not necessarily improve the heart. It would be an error to say that it has no effect. It throws certain seeds of thought into the *antaḥkaraṇa* and, if these thoughts become habitual, they influence the conduct. But the danger of moral text-books is that they make the thinking of high things mechanical and artificial, and whatever is mechanical and artificial is inoperative for good.

There are three things which are of the utmost importance in dealing with a man's moral nature, the emotions, the *saṁskāras* or formed habits and associations, and the *svabhāva* or nature. The only way for him to train himself morally is to habituate himself to the right emotions, the noblest associations, the best mental, emotional and physical habits and the following out in right action of the fundamental impulses of his essential nature. You can impose a certain discipline on children, dress them into a certain mould, lash them into a desired path, but unless you can get their hearts and natures on your side, the conformity to this imposed rule becomes a hypocritical and heartless, a conventional, often a cowardly compliance. This is what is done in Europe, and it leads to that remarkable phenomenon known as the sowing of wild oats as soon as the yoke of discipline at school and at home is removed, and to the social hypocrisy which is so large a feature of European life. Only what the man admires and accepts, becomes part of himself; the rest is a mask. He conforms to the discipline of society as he conformed to the moral routine of home and school, but considers himself at liberty to guide his real life, inner and private, according to his own likings and passions. On the other hand, to neglect moral and religious education altogether is to corrupt the race. The notorious moral corruption in our young men previous to the saving touch of the Swadeshi movement was the direct result of the purely mental instruction given to them under the English system of education. The adoption of the English system under an Indian disguise in institutions like the Central Hindu College is likely to lead to the European result. That it is better than nothing, is all that can be said for it.

As in the education of the mind, so in the education of the heart, the best way is to put the child into the right road to his own perfection and encourage him to follow it, watching, suggesting, helping, but not interfering. The one excellent element in the English boarding school is that the master at his best stands there as a moral guide and example, leaving the boys largely to influence and help each other in following the path silently shown to them. But the method practised is crude and marred by the excess of outer discipline, for which the pupils have no respect except that of fear, and the exiguity of the inner assistance. The little good that is done is outweighed by much evil. The old Indian system of the *guru* commanding by his knowledge and sanctity the implicit obedience, perfect admiration, reverent emulation of the student was a far superior method of moral discipline. It is impossible to restore that ancient system; but it is not impossible to substitute the wise friend, guide and helper for the hired instructor or the benevolent policeman which is all that the European system usually makes of the pedagogue.

The first rule of moral training is to suggest and invite, not command or impose. The best method of suggestion is by personal example, daily converse and the books read from day to day. These books should contain, for the younger student, the lofty examples of the past given, not as moral lessons, but as things of supreme human interest, and, for the elder student, the great thoughts of great souls, the passages of literature which set fire to the highest emotions and prompt the highest ideals and aspirations, the records of history and biography which exemplify the living of those great thoughts, noble emotions and aspiring ideals. This is a kind of good company, *satsanga*, which can seldom fail to have effect so long as sententious sermonising is avoided, and becomes of the highest effect if the personal life of the teacher is itself moulded by the great things he places before his pupils. It cannot, however, have full force unless the young life is given an opportunity, within its limited sphere, of embodying in action the moral impulses which rise within it. The thirst of knowledge, the self-devotion, the purity, the renunciation of the Brahmin, — the courage, ardour, honour, nobility, chivalry, patriotism. of the Kshatriya,

— the beneficence, skill, industry, generous enterprise and large open-handedness of the Vaisya, — the self-effacement and loving service of the Sudra, — these are the qualities of the Aryan. They constitute the moral temper we desire in our young men, in the whole nation. But how can we get them if we do not give opportunities to the young to train themselves in the Aryan tradition, to form by the practice and familiarity of childhood and boyhood the stuff of which their adult lives must be made?

Every boy should, therefore, be given practical opportunity as well as intellectual encouragement to develop all that is best in the nature. If he has bad qualities, bad habits, bad *saṁskāras*, whether of mind or body, he should not be treated harshly as a delinquent, but encouraged to get rid of them by the Rajayogic method of *saṁyama*, rejection and substitution. He should be encouraged to think of them not as sins or offences, but as symptoms of a curable disease, alterable by a steady and sustained effort of the will, — falsehood being rejected whenever it rises into the mind and replaced by truth, fear by courage, selfishness by sacrifice and renunciation, malice by love. Great care will have to be taken that unformed virtues are not rejected as faults. The wildness and recklessness of many young natures are only the overflowings of an excessive strength, greatness and nobility. They should be purified, not discouraged.

I have spoken of morality; it is necessary to speak a word of religious teaching. There is a strange idea prevalent that by merely teaching the dogmas of religion children can be made pious and moral. This is an European error, and its practice either leads to mechanical acceptance of a creed having no effect on the inner and little on the outer life, or it creates the fanatic, the pietist, the ritualist or the unctuous hypocrite. Religion has to be lived, not learned as a creed. The singular compromise made in the so-called National Education of Bengal making the teaching of religious beliefs compulsory, but forbidding the practice of *anuṣṭhāna* or religious exercise, is a sample of the ignorant confusion which distracts men's minds on this subject. The prohibition is a sop to secularism declared or concealed. No religious teaching is of any value unless it is lived, and the use of various kinds of *sādhanā*, spiritual self-training and exercise is the only effective preparation for religious living. The ritual of prayer, homage, ceremony is craved for by many minds as an essential preparation and, if not made an end in itself, is a great help to spiritual progress; if it is withheld, some other form of meditation, devotion or religious duty must be put in its place. Otherwise, religious teaching is of little use and would almost be better ungiven.

But whether distinct teaching in any form of religion is imparted or not, the essence of religion, to live for God, for humanity, for country, for others and for oneself in these, must be made the ideal in every school which calls itself national. It is this spirit of Hinduism pervading our schools which — far more than the teaching of Indian subjects, the use of Indian methods or formal instruction in Hindu beliefs and Hindu scriptures — should be the essence of Nationalism in our schools distinguishing them from all others.

IV

SIMULTANEOUS AND SUCCESSIVE TEACHING

A very remarkable feature of modern training which has been subjected in India to a *reductio ad absurdum* is the practice of teaching by snippets. A subject is taught a little at a time, in conjunction with a host of others, with the result that what might be well learnt in a single year is badly learned in seven and the boy goes out ill-equipped, served with imperfect parcels of knowledge, master of none of the great departments of human knowledge. The system of education adopted by the National Council, an amphibious and twy-natured creation, attempts to heighten this practice of teaching by snippets at the bottom and the middle and suddenly change it to a grandiose specialism at the top. This is to base the triangle on its apex and hope that it will stand.

The old system was to teach one or two subjects well and thoroughly and then proceed to others, and certainly it was a more rational system than the modern. If it did not impart so much varied information, it built up a deeper, nobler and more real culture. Much of the shallowness, discursive lightness and fickle mutability of the average modern mind is due to the vicious principle of teaching by snippets. The one defect that can be alleged against the old system was that the subject earliest learned might fade from the mind of the student while he was mastering his later studies. But the excellent training given to the memory by the ancients obviated the incidence of this defect. In the future education we need not bind ourselves either by the ancient or the modern system, but select only the most perfect and rapid means of mastering knowledge.

In defence of the modern system it is alleged that the attention of children is easily tired and cannot be subjected to the strain of long application to a single subject. The frequent change of subject gives rest to the mind. The question naturally arises: are the children of modern times then so different from the ancients, and, if so, have we not made them so by discouraging prolonged concentration? A very young child cannot, indeed, apply himself; but a very young child is unfit for school teaching of any kind. A child of seven or eight, and that is the earliest permissible age for the commencement of any regular kind of study, is capable of a good deal of concentration if he is interested. Interest is, after all, the basis of concentration. We make his lessons supremely uninteresting and repellent to the child, a harsh compulsion the basis of teaching and then complain of his restless inattention! The substitution of a natural self-education by the child for the present unnatural system will remove this objection of inability. A child, like a man, if he is interested, much prefers to get to the end of its subject rather than leave it unfinished. To lead him on step by step, interesting and absorbing him in each as it comes, until he has mastered his subject is the true art of teaching.

The first attention of the teacher must be given to the medium and the instruments, and, until these are perfected, to multiply subjects of regular instruction is to waste time and energy. When the mental instruments are sufficiently developed to acquire a language easily and swiftly, that is the time to introduce him to many languages, not when he can only partially understand what he is taught and masters it laboriously and imperfectly. Moreover, one who has mastered his own language, has one very necessary facility for mastering another. With the linguistic faculty unsatisfactorily developed in one's own tongue, to master others is impossible. To study science with the faculties of observation, judgment, reasoning and comparison only slightly developed is to undertake a useless and thankless labour. So it is with all other subjects.

The mother-tongue is the proper medium of education and therefore the first energies of the child should be directed to the thorough mastering of the medium. Almost every child has an imagination, an instinct for words, a dramatic faculty, a wealth of idea and fancy. These should be interested in the literature and history of the nation. Instead of stupid and dry spelling and reading books, looked on as a dreary and ungrateful task, he should be introduced by rapidly progressive stages to the most interesting parts of his own literature and the life around him and behind him, and they should be put before him in such a way as to attract and appeal to the qualities of which I have spoken. All other study at this period should be devoted to the perfection of the mental functions and the moral character. A foundation should be laid at this time for the study of history, science, philosophy, art, but not in an obtrusive and formal manner. Every child is a lover of interesting narrative, a hero-worshipper and a patriot. Appeal to these qualities in him and through them let him master without knowing it the living and human parts of his nation's history. Every child is an enquirer, an investigator, analyser, a merciless anatomist. Appeal to those qualities in him and let him acquire without knowing it the right temper and the necessary fundamental knowledge of the scientist. Every child has an insatiable intellectual curiosity and turn for metaphysical enquiry. Use it to draw him on slowly to an understanding of the world and himself. Every child has the gift of imitation and a touch of imaginative power. Use it to give him the groundwork of the faculty of the artist.

It is by allowing Nature to work that we get the benefit of the gifts she has bestowed on us. Humanity in its education of children has chosen to thwart and hamper her processes and, by so doing, has done much to thwart and hamper the rapidity of its onward march. Happily, saner ideas are now beginning to prevail. But the way has not yet been found. The past hangs about our necks with all its prejudices and errors and will not leave us: it enters into our most radical attempts to return to the guidance of the all-wise Mother. We must have the courage to take up clearer knowledge and apply it fearlessly in the interests of posterity. Teaching by snippets must be relegated to the lumber-room of dead sorrows. The first work is to interest the child in life, work and knowledge, to develop his instruments of knowledge with the utmost thoroughness, to give him mastery of the medium he must use. Afterwards, the rapidity with which he will learn will make up for any delay in taking up regular studies, and it will be found that, where now he learns a few things badly, then he will learn many things thoroughly well.

V

THE TRAINING OF THE SENSES

There are six senses which minister to knowledge, sight, hearing, smell, touch and taste, mind, and all of these except the last look outward and gather the material of thought from outside through the physical nerves and their end-organs, eye, ear, nose, skin, palate. The perfection of the senses as ministers to thought must be one of the first cares of the teacher. The two things that are needed of the senses are accuracy and sensitiveness. We must first understand what are the obstacles to the accuracy and sensitiveness of the senses, in order that we may take the best steps to remove them. The cause of imperfection must be understood by those who desire to bring about perfection.

The senses depend for their accuracy and sensitiveness on the unobstructed activity of the nerves which are the channels of their information and the passive acceptance of the mind which is the recipient. In themselves the organs do their work perfectly. The eye gives the right form, the ear the correct sound, the palate the right taste, the skin the right touch, the nose the right smell. This can easily be understood if we study the action of the eye as a crucial example. A correct image is reproduced automatically on the retina; if there is any error in appreciating it, it is not the fault of the organ, but of something else.

The fault may be with the nerve currents. The nerves are nothing but channels, they have no power in themselves to alter the information given by the organs. But a channel may be obstructed and the obstruction may interfere either with the fullness or the accuracy of the information, not as it reaches the organ where it is necessarily and automatically perfect, but as it reaches the mind. The only exception is in case of a physical defect in the organ as an instrument. That is not a matter for the educationist, but for the physician.

If the obstruction is such as to stop the information reaching the mind at all, the result is an insufficient sensitiveness of the senses. The defects of sight, hearing, smell, touch, taste, anaesthesia in its various degrees, are curable when not the effect of physical injury or defect in the organ itself. The obstructions can be removed and the sensitiveness remedied by the purification of the nerve system. The remedy is a simple one which is now becoming more and more popular in Europe for different reasons and objects, the regulation of the breathing. This process inevitably restores the perfect and unobstructed activity of the channels and, if well and thoroughly done, leads to a high activity of the senses. The process is called in Yogic discipline *naḍi-śuddhi* or nerve-purification.

The obstruction in the channel may be such as not absolutely to stop in however small a degree, but to distort the information. A familiar instance of this is the effect of fear or alarm on the sense action. The startled horse takes the sack on the road for a dangerous living thing, the startled man takes a rope for a snake, a waving curtain for a ghostly form. All distortions due to actions in the nervous system can be traced to some kind of emotional disturbance acting in the nerve channels. The only remedy for them is the habit of calm, the habitual steadiness of the nerves. This also can be brought about by *naḍi-śuddhi* or nerve-purification, which quiets the system, gives a deliberate calmness to all the internal processes and prepares the purification of the mind.

If the nerve channels are quiet and clear, the only possible disturbance of the information is from or through the mind. Now the *manas* or sixth sense is in itself a channel like the nerves, a channel for communication with the *buddhi* or brain-force. Disturbance may happen either from above or from below. The information outside is first photographed on the end organ, then reproduced at the other end of the nerve system in the *citta* or passive memory. All the images of sight, sound, smell, touch and taste are deposited there and the *manas* reports them to the *buddhi*. The *manas* is both a sense organ and a channel. As a sense organ it is as automatically perfect as the others, as a channel it is subject to disturbance resulting either in obstruction or distortion.

As a sense organ the mind receives direct thought impressions from outside and from within. These impressions are in themselves perfectly correct, but in their report to the intellect they may either not reach the intellect at all or may reach it so distorted as to make a false or partially false impression. The disturbance may affect the impression which attends the information of eye, ear, nose, skin or palate, but it is very slightly powerful here. In its effect on the direct impressions of the mind, it is extremely powerful and the chief source of error. The mind takes direct impressions primarily of thought, but also of form, sound, indeed of all the things for which it usually prefers to depend on the sense organs. The full development of this sensitiveness of the mind is called in our Yogic discipline *sūkṣmadṛṣṭi* or subtle reception of images. Telepathy, clairvoyance, clairaudience, presentiment, thought-reading, character-reading and many other modern discoveries are very ancient powers of the mind which have been left undeveloped, and they all belong to the *manas*. The development of the sixth sense has never formed part of human training. In a future age it will undoubtedly take a place in the necessary preliminary training of the human instrument. Meanwhile there is no reason why the mind should not be trained to give a correct report to the intellect so that our thought may start with absolutely correct if not with full impressions.

The first obstacle, the nervous-emotional, we may suppose to be removed by the purification of the nervous system. The second obstacle is that of the emotions themselves warping the impression as it comes. Love may do this, hatred may do this, any emotion or desire according to its power and intensity may distort the impression as it travels. This difficulty can only be removed by the discipline of the emotions, the purifying of the moral habits. This is a part of moral training and its consideration may be postponed for the moment. The next difficulty is the interference of previous associations formed or ingrained in the *citta* or passive memory. We have a habitual way of looking at things and the conservative inertia in our nature disposes us to give every new experience the shape and semblance of those to which we are accustomed. It is only more developed minds which can receive first impressions without an unconscious bias against the novelty of novel experience. For instance, if we get a true impression of what is happening — and we habitually act on such impressions true or false — if it differs from what we are accustomed to expect, the old association meets it in the *citta* and sends a changed report to the intellect in which either the new impression is overlaid and concealed by the old or mingled with it. To go farther into this subject would be to involve ourselves too deeply into the details of psychology. This typical instance will suffice. To get rid of this obstacle is impossible without *citta-śuddhi* or purification of the mental and moral habits formed in the *citta*. This is a preliminary process of Yoga and was effected in our ancient system by various means, but would be considered out of place in a modern system of education.

It is clear, therefore, that unless we revert to our old Indian system in some of its principles, we must be content to allow this source of disturbance to remain. A really national system of education would not allow itself to be controlled by European ideas in this all-important matter. And there is a process so simple and momentous that it can easily be made a part of our system.

It consists in bringing about passivity of the restless flood of thought-sensations rising of its own momentum from the passive memory independent of our will and control. This passivity liberates the intellect from the siege of old associations and false impressions. It gives it power to select only what is wanted from the storehouse of the passive memory, automatically brings about the habit of getting right impressions and enables the intellect to dictate to the *citta* what *saṁskāras* or associations shall be formed or rejected. This is the real office of the intellect, — to discriminate, choose, select, arrange. But so long as there is not *citta-śuddhi*, instead of doing this office perfectly, it itself remains imperfect and corrupt and adds to the confusion in the mind channel by false judgment, false imagination, false memory, false observation, false comparison, contrast and analogy, false deduction, induction and inference. The purification of the *citta* is essential for the liberation, purification and perfect action of the intellect.

VI

SENSE-IMPROVEMENT BY PRACTICE

Another cause of the inefficiency of the senses as gatherers of knowledge, is insufficient use. We do not observe sufficiently or with sufficient attention and closeness and a sight, sound, smell, even touch or taste knocks in vain at the door for admission. This *tāmasic* inertia of the receiving instruments is no doubt due to the inattention of the *buddhi*, and therefore its consideration may seem to come properly under the training of the functions of the intellect, but it is more convenient, though less psychologically correct, to notice it here. The student ought to be accustomed to catch the sights, sounds, etc., around him, distinguish them, mark their nature, properties and sources and fix them in the *citta* so that they may be always ready to respond when called for by the memory.

It is a fact which has been proved by minute experiments that the faculty of observation is very imperfectly developed in men, merely from want of care in the use of the sense and the memory. Give twelve men the task of recording from memory something they all saw two hours ago and the accounts will all vary from each other and from the actual occurrence. To get rid of this imperfection will go a long way towards the removal of error. It can be done by training the senses to do their work perfectly, which they will do readily enough if they know the *buddhi* requires it of them, and giving sufficient attention to put the facts in their right place and order in the memory.

Attention is a factor in knowledge, the importance of

which has been always recognised. Attention is the first condition of right memory and of accuracy. To attend to what he is doing is the first element of discipline required of the student, and, as I have suggested, this can easily be secured if the object of attention is made interesting. This attention to a single thing is called concentration. One truth is, however, sometimes overlooked: that concentration on several things at a time is often indispensable. When people talk of concentration, they imply centring the mind on one thing at a time; but it is quite possible to develop the power of double concentration, triple concentration, multiple concentration. When a given incident is happening, it may be made up of several simultaneous happenings or a set of simultaneous circumstances, a sight, a sound, a touch or several sights, sounds, touches occurring at the same moment or in the same short space of time. The tendency of the mind is to fasten on one and mark others vaguely, many not at all or, if compelled to attend to all, to be distracted and mark none perfectly. Yet this can be remedied and the attention equally distributed over a set of circumstances in such a way as to observe and remember each perfectly. It is merely a matter of *abhyāsa* or steady natural practice.

It is also very desirable that the hand should be capable of coming to the help of the eye in dealing with the multitudinous objects of its activity so as to ensure accuracy. This is of a use so obvious and imperatively needed, that it need not be dwelt on at length. The practice of imitation by the hand of the thing seen is of use both in detecting the lapses and inaccuracies of the mind, in noticing the objects of sense and in registering accurately what has been seen. Imitation by the hand ensures accuracy of observation. This is one of the first uses of drawing and it is sufficient in itself to make the teaching of this subject a necessary part of the training of the organs.

VII

THE TRAINING OF THE MENTAL FACULTIES

The first qualities of the mind that have to be developed are those which can be grouped under observation. We notice some things, ignore others. Even of what we notice, we observe very little. A general perception of an object is what we all usually carry away from a cursory half-attentive glance. A closer attention fixes its place, form, nature as distinct from its surroundings. Full concentration of the faculty of observation gives us all the knowledge that the three chief senses can gather about the object, or if we touch or taste, we may gather all that the five senses can tell of its nature and properties. Those who make use of the sixth sense, the poet, the painter, the Yogin, can also gather much that is hidden from the ordinary observer. The scientist by investigation ascertains other facts open to a minuter observation. These are the components of the faculty of observation, and it is obvious that its basis is attention, which may be only close or close and minute. We may gather much even from a passing glance at an object, if we have the habit of concentrating the attention and the habit of *sāttwic* receptivity. The first thing the teacher has to do is to accustom the pupil to concentrate attention.

We may take the instance of a flower. Instead of looking casually at it and getting a casual impression of scent, form and colour, he should be encouraged to know the flower — to fix in his mind the exact shade, the peculiar glow, the precise intensity of the scent, the beauty of curve and design in the form. His touch should assure itself of the texture and its peculiarities. Next, the flower should be taken to pieces and its structure examined with the same carefulness of observation. All this should be done not as a task, but as an object of interest by skilfully arranged questions suited to the learner which will draw him on to observe and investigate one thing after the other until he has almost unconsciously mastered the whole.

Memory and judgment are the next qualities that will be called upon, and they should be encouraged in the same unconscious way. The student should not be made to repeat the same lesson over again in order to remember it. That is a mechanical, burdensome and unintelligent way of training the memory. A similar but different flower should be put in the hands and he should be encouraged to note it with the same care, but with the avowed object of noting the similarities and differences. By this practice daily repeated the memory will naturally be trained. Not only so, but the mental centres of comparison and contrast will be developed. The learner will begin to observe as a habit the similarities of things and their differences. The teacher should take every care to encourage the perfect growth of this faculty and habit. At the same time, the laws of species and genus will begin to dawn on the mind and, by a skilful following and leading of the young developing mind, the scientific habit, the scientific attitude and the fundamental facts of scientific knowledge may in a very short time be made part of its permanent equipment. The observation and comparison of flowers, leaves, plants, trees will lay the foundations of botanical knowledge without loading the mind with names and that dry set acquisition of informations which is the beginning of cramming and detested by the healthy human mind when it is fresh from nature and un-

spoiled by unnatural habits. In the same way by the observation of the stars, astronomy, by the observation of earth,
stones, etc., geology, by the observation of insects and animals, entomology and zoology may be founded. A little
later chemistry may be started by interesting observation of
experiments without any formal teaching or heaping on the
mind of formulas and book-knowledge. There is no scientific subject the perfect and natural mastery of which cannot
be prepared in early childhood by this training of the faculties to observe, compare, remember and judge various classes
of objects. It can be done easily and attended with a supreme
and absorbing interest in the mind of the student. Once the
taste is created, the boy can be trusted to follow it up with
all the enthusiasm of youth in his leisure hours. This will
prevent the necessity at a later age of teaching him everything in class.

The judgment will naturally be trained along with the
other faculties. At every step the boy will have to decide
what is the right idea, measurement, appreciation of colour,
sound, scent, etc., and what is the wrong. Often the judgments and distinctions made will have to be exceedingly
subtle and delicate. At first many errors will be made, but
the learner should be taught to trust his judgment without
being attached to its results. It will be found that the judgment will soon begin to respond to the calls made on it,
clear itself of all errors and begin to judge correctly and
minutely. The best way is to accustom the boy to compare
his judgments with those of others. When he is wrong, it
should at first be pointed out to him how far he was right
and why he went wrong; afterwards he should be encouraged to note these things for himself. Every time he is
right, his attention should be prominently and encoura-

gingly called to it so that he may get confidence.

While engaged in comparing and contrasting, another centre is certain to develop, the centre of analogy. The learner will inevitably draw analogies and argue from like to like. He should be encouraged to use this faculty while noticing its limitations and errors. In this way he will be trained to form the habit of correct analogy which is an indispensable aid in the acquisition of knowledge.

The one faculty we have omitted, apart from the faculty of direct reasoning, is Imagination. This is a most important and indispensable instrument. It may be divided into three functions, the forming of mental images, the power of creating thoughts, images and imitations or new combinations of existing thoughts and images, the appreciation of the soul in things, beauty, charm, greatness, hidden suggestiveness, the emotion and spiritual life that pervades the world. This is in every way as important as the training of the faculties which observe and compare outward things. But that demands a separate and fuller treatment.

The mental faculties should first be exercised on things, afterwards on words and ideas. Our dealings with language are much too perfunctory and the absence of a fine sense for words impoverishes the intellect and limits the fineness and truth of its operation. The mind should be accustomed first to notice the word thoroughly, its form, sound and sense; then to compare the form with other similar forms in the points of similarity and difference, thus forming the foundation of the grammatical sense; then to distinguish between the fine shades of sense of similar words and the formation and rhythm of different sentences, thus forming the foundation of the literary and the syntactical faculties. All this should be done informally, drawing on the curiosity and interest, avoiding set teaching and memorising of rules. The true knowledge takes its base on things, *arthas*, and only when it has mastered the thing, proceeds to formalise its information.

VIII

THE TRAINING OF THE LOGICAL FACULTY

The training of the logical reason must necessarily follow the training of the faculties which collect the material on which the logical reason must work. Not only so but the mind must have some development of the faculty of dealing with words before it can deal successfully with ideas. The question is, once this preliminary work is done, what is the best way of teaching the boy to think correctly from premises. For the logical reason cannot proceed without premises. It either infers from facts to a conclusion, or from previously formed conclusions to a fresh one, or from one fact to another. It either induces, deduces or simply infers. I see the sunrise day after day, I conclude or induce that it rises as a law daily after a varying interval of darkness. I have already ascertained that wherever there is smoke, there is fire. I have induced that general rule from an observation of facts. I deduce that in a particular case of smoke there is a fire behind. I infer that a man must have lit it from the improbability of any other cause under the particular circumstances. I cannot deduce it because fire is not always created by human kindling; it may be volcanic or caused by a stroke of lightning or the sparks from some kind of friction in the neighbourhood.

There are three elements necessary to correct reasoning: first, the correctness of the facts or conclusions I start from, secondly, the completeness as well as the accuracy of the data I start from, thirdly, the elimination of other possible or impossible conclusions from the same facts. The fallibility of the logical reason is due partly to avoidable negligence and looseness in securing these conditions, partly to the difficulty of getting all the facts correct, still more to the difficulty of getting all the facts complete, most of all, to the extreme difficulty of eliminating all possible conclusions except the one which happens to be right. No fact is supposed to be more perfectly established than the universality of the Law of Gravitation as an imperative rule, yet a single new fact inconsistent with it would upset this supposed universality. And such facts exist. Nevertheless by care and keenness the fallibility may be reduced to its minimum.

The usual practice is to train the logical reason by teaching the science of Logic. This is an instance of the prevalent error by which book-knowledge of a thing is made the object of the study instead of the thing itself. The experience of reasoning and its errors should be given to the mind and it should be taught to observe how these work for itself; it should proceed from the example to the rule and from the accumulating harmony of rules to the formal science of the subject, not from the formal science to the rule, and from the rule to the example.

The first step is to make the young mind interest itself in drawing inferences from the facts, tracing cause and effect. It should then be led on to notice its successes and its failures and the reasons of the success and of the failure: the incorrectness of the fact started from, the haste in drawing conclusions from insufficient facts, the carelessness in accepting a conclusion which is improbable, little supported by the data or open to doubt, the indolence or prejudice which does not wish to onsider other possible explanations or conclusions. In this way the mind can be trained to reason as correctly as the fallibility of human logic will allow, minimising the chances of error. The study of formal logic should be postponed to a later time when it can easily be mastered in a very brief period, since it will be only the systematising of an art perfectly well known to the student.

Education — Intellectual

This incomplete article was found among Sri Aurobindo's early manuscripts (Baroda 1893-1906). The opening sentence clearly suggests that there were other articles in the series. These, however, have not been traced so far.

EDUCATION — INTELLECTUAL

We now come to the intellectual part of education, which is certainly a larger and more difficult, although not more important than physical training and edification of character. The Indian University system has confined itself entirely to this branch and it might have been thought that this limitation and concentration of energy ought to have been attended by special efficiency and thoroughness in the single branch it had chosen. But unfortunately this is not the case. If the physical training it provides is contemptible and the moral training nil, the mental training is also meagre in quantity and worthless in quality. People commonly say that it is because the services and professions are made the object of education that this state of things exists. This I believe to be a great mistake. A degree is necessary for service and therefore people try to get a degree. Good! let it remain so. But in order for a student to get a degree let us make it absolutely necessary that he shall have a good education. If a worthless education is sufficient in order to secure this object and a good education quite unessential, it is obvious that the student will not incur great trouble and diversion of energy in order to acquire what he feels to be unnecessary. But change this state of things, make culture and true science essential and the same interested motive which now makes him content with a bad education will then compel him to strive after culture and true science. As practical men we must recognise that the pure enthusiasm of knowledge for knowledge's sake operates only in exceptional minds or in exceptional eras. In civilised countries a general desire for knowledge as a motive for education does exist but it is largely accompanied with the earthier feeling that knowledge is necessary to keep up one's position in society or to succeed in certain lucrative or respectable pursuits or professions. We in India have become so barbarous that we send our children to school with the grossest utilitarian motive unmixed with any disinterested desire for knowledge; but the education we receive is itself responsible for this. Nobody can cherish disinterested enthusiasm for a bad education; it can only be regarded as a means to some practical end. But make the education good, thorough and interesting and the love of knowledge will of itself awake in the mind and so mingle with and modify more selfish objects.

The source of the evil we complain of is therefore something different; it is a fundamental and deplorable error by which we in this country have confused education with the acquisition of knowledge and interpreted knowledge itself in a singularly narrow and illiberal sense. To give the student knowledge is necessary, but it is still more necessary to build up in him the power of knowledge. It would hardly be a good technical education for a carpenter to be taught how to fell trees so as to provide himself with wood and never to learn how to prepare tables and chairs and cabinets or even what tools were necessary for his craft. Yet this is precisely what our system of education does. It trains the memory and provides the student with a store of facts and second-hand ideas. The memory is the woodcutter's axe and the store he acquires is the wood he has cut down in his course of tree-felling. When he has done this, the University says to him, "We now declare you a Bachelor of Carpentry, we have given you a good and sharp axe and a fair nucleus of wood to begin with. Go on, my son, the world is full of forests and, provided the Forest Officer does not object, you can cut down trees and provide yourself with wood to your heart's content." Now the student who goes forth thus equipped, may become a great timber merchant but, unless he is an exceptional genius, he will never be even a moderate carpenter. Or to return from the simile to the facts, the graduate from our colleges may be a good clerk, a decent vakil or a tolerable medical practitioner, but unless he is an exceptional genius, he will never be a great administrator or a great lawyer or an eminent medical specialist. These eminences have to be filled up mainly by Europeans. If an Indian wishes to rise to them, he has to travel thousands of miles over the sea in order to breathe an atmosphere of liberal knowledge, original science and sound culture. And even then he seldom succeeds, because his lungs are too debilitated to take in a good long breath of that atmosphere.

The first fundamental mistake has been, therefore, to confine ourselves to the training of the storing faculty memory and the storage of facts and to neglect the training of the three great using (manipulating) faculties, viz. the power of reasoning, the power of comparison and differentiation and the power of expression. These powers are present to a certain extent in all men above the state of the savage and even in a rudimentary state in the savage himself; but they exist especially developed in the higher classes of civilised nations, wherever these higher classes have long centuries of education behind them. But however highly developed by nature these powers demand cultivation, they demand that bringing out of natural abilities which is the real essence of education. If not brought out in youth, they become rusted and stopped with dirt, so that they cease to act except in a feeble, narrow and partial manner. Exceptional genius does indeed assert itself in spite of neglect and discouragement, but even genius self-developed does not achieve as happy results and as free and large a working as the same genius properly equipped and trained. Amount of knowledge is in itself not of first importance, but to make the best use of what we know. The easy assumption of our educationists that we have only to supply the mind with a smattering of facts in each department of knowledge and the mind can be trusted to develop itself and take its own suitable road is contrary to science, contrary to human experience and contrary to the universal opinion of civilised countries. Indeed, the history of intellectual degeneration in gifted races always begins with the arrest of these three mental powers by the excessive cultivation of mere knowledge at their expense. Much as we have lost as a nation, we have always preserved our intellectual alertness, quickness and originality; but even this last gift is threatened by our University system, and if it goes, it will be the beginning of irretrievable degradation and final extinction.

The very first step in reform must therefore be to revolutionise the whole aim and method of our education. We must accustom teachers to devote nine-tenths of their energy to the education of the active mental faculties while the passive and retaining faculty, which we call the memory, should occupy a recognised and well-defined but subordinate place and we must direct our school and university examinations to the testing of these active faculties and not of the memory. For this is an object which cannot be affected by the mere change or rearrangement of the curriculum. It is true that certain subjects are more apt to develop certain faculties than others; the power of accurate reasoning is powerfully assisted by Geometry, Logic and Political Economy; one of the most important results of languages is to refine and train the power of expression and nothing more enlarges the power of comparison and differentiation than an intelligent study of history. But no particular subject except language is essential, still less exclusively appropriate to any given faculty. There are types of intellect, for instance, which are constitutionally incapable of dealing with geometrical problems or even with the formal machinery of Logic, and are yet profound, brilliant and correct reasoners in other intellectual spheres. There is in fact hardly any subject, the sciences of calculation excepted, which in the hands of a capable teacher does not give room for the development of all the general faculties of the mind. The first thing needed therefore is the entire and unsparing rejection of the present methods of teaching in favour of those which are now being universally adopted in the more advanced countries of Europe.

But even in this narrower sphere of knowledge acquisition to which our system has confined itself, it has been guilty of other blunders quite as serious. Apart from pure mathematics, which stands on a footing of its own, knowledge may be divided into two great heads, the knowledge of things and the knowledge of men, that is to say, of human thought, human actions, human nature and human creations as recorded, preserved or pictured in literature, history, philosophy and art. The latter is covered in the term humanities or humane letters and the idea of a liberal education was formerly confined to these, though it was subsequently widened to include mathematics and has again been widened in modern times to include a modicum of science. The humanities, mathematics and science are therefore the three sisters in the family of knowledge and any self-respecting system of education must in these days provide facilities for mastery in any one of these as well as for a modicum of all. The first great error of our system comes in here. While we insist on passing our students through a rigid and cast-iron course of knowledge in everything, we give them real knowledge in nothing. Mathematics, for instance, is a subject in which it ought not to be difficult to give thorough knowledge, most of the paths are well beaten and, being a precise and definite subject, it does not in itself demand such serious powers of original thought and appreciation as literature and history; yet it is the invariable experience of the most brilliant mathematical students who go from Calcutta or Bombay to Cambridge that after the first year they have exhausted all they have already learned and have to enter on entirely new and unfamiliar result. It is surely a deplorable thing that it should be impossible to acquire a thorough mathematical education in India, that one should have to go thousands of miles and spend thousands of rupees to get it. Again, if we look at science, what is the result of the pitiful modicum of science acquired under our system? At the best it turns out good teachers who can turn others through the same mill in which they themselves have been ground...

(Incomplete)

Message

★

Perfection of the Body

Sri Aurobindo wrote a series of eight articles
— the last of his prose writings — for the
Bulletin of Physical Education (later called the
*Bulletin of Sri Aurobindo International Centre
of Education*), a quarterly journal started in
February 1949. These two articles appeared in
the first two issues — February and April 1949
— of the periodical.

MESSAGE

I take the opportunity of the publication of this issue of the "Bulletin d'Education Physique" of the Ashram to give my blessings to the Journal and the Association — J.S.A.S.A. (Jeunesse Sportive de l'Ashram de Sri Aurobindo). In doing so I would like to dwell for a while on the deeper raison d'être of such Associations and especially the need and utility for the nation of a wide-spread organisation of them and such sports or physical exercises as are practised here. In their more superficial aspect they appear merely as games and amusements which people take up for entertainment or as a field for the outlet of the body's energy and natural instinct of activity or for a means of the development and maintenance of the health and strength of the body; but they are or can be much more than that: they are also fields for the development of habits, capacities and qualities which are greatly needed and of the utmost service to a people in war or in peace, and in its political and social activities, in most indeed of the provinces of a combined human endeavour. It is to this which we may call the national aspect of the subject that I would wish to give especial prominence.

In our own time these sports, games and athletics have assumed a place and command a general interest such as was seen only in earlier times in countries like Greece, Greece where all sides of human activity were equally developed and the gymnasium, chariot-racing and other sports and athletics had the same importance on the physical side as on the mental side the Arts and poetry and the drama, and were especially stimulated and attended to by the civic authorities of the City State. It was Greece that made an institution of the Olympiad and the recent re-establishment of the Olympiad as an international institution is a significant sign of the revival of the ancient spirit. This kind of interest has spread to a certain extent to our own country and India has begun to take a place in international contests such as the Olympiad. The newly founded State in liberated India is also beginning to be interested in developing all sides of the life of the nation and is likely to take an active part and a habit of direction in fields which were formerly left to private initiative. It is taking up, for instance, the question of the foundation and preservation of health and physical fitness in the nation and in the spreading of a general recognition of its importance. It is in this connection that the encouragement of sports and associations for athletics and all activities of this kind would be an incalculable assistance. A generalisation of the habit of taking part in such exercises in childhood and youth and early manhood would help greatly towards the creation of physically fit and energetic people.

But of a higher import than the foundation, however necessary, of health, strength and fitness of the body is the development of discipline and morale and sound and strong character towards which these activities can help. There are many sports which are of the utmost value towards this end, because they help to form and even necessitate the qualities of courage, hardihood, energetic action and initiative or call for skill, steadiness of will or rapid decision and action, the perception of what is to be done in an emergency and dexterity in doing it. One development of the utmost value is the awakening of the essential and instinctive body consciousness which can see and do what is necessary without any indication from mental thought and which is equivalent in the body to swift insight in the mind and spontaneous and

rapid decision in the will. One may add the formation of a
capacity for harmonious and right movements of the body,
especially in a combined action, economic of physical effort
and discouraging waste of energy, which result from such
exercises as marches or drill and which displace the loose and
straggling, the inharmonious or disorderly or wasteful
movements common to the untrained individual body.
Another invaluable result of these activities is the growth of
what has been called the sporting spirit. That includes good
humour and tolerance and consideration for all, a right
attitude and friendliness to competitors and rivals, self-
control and scrupulous observance of the laws of the game,
fair play and avoidance of the use of foul means, an equal
acceptance of victory or defeat without bad humour, resentment or ill-will towards successful competitors, loyal acceptance of the decisions of the appointed judge, umpire or
referee. These qualities have their value for life in general
and not only for sport, but the help that sport can give to
their development is direct and invaluable. If they could be
made more common not only in the life of the individual but
in the national life and in the international where at the
present day the opposite tendencies have become too ram-
pant, existence in this troubled world of ours would be
smoother and might open to a greater chance of concord
and amity of which it stands very much in need. More
important still is the custom of discipline, obedience, order,
habit of team-work, which certain games necessitate. For
without them success is uncertain or impossible. Innu-
merable are the activities in life, especially in national
life, in which leadership and obedience to leadership in
combined action are necessary for success, victory in combat or fulfilment of a purpose. The role of the leader, the

captain, the power and skill of his leadership, his ability to command the confidence and ready obedience of his followers is of the utmost importance in all kinds of combined action or enterprise; but few can develop these things without having learnt themselves to obey and to act as one mind or as one body with others. This strictness of training, this habit of discipline and obedience is not inconsistent with individual freedom; it is often the necessary condition for its right use, just as order is not inconsistent with liberty but rather the condition for the right use of liberty and even for its preservation and survival. In all kinds of concerted action this rule is indispensable: orchestration becomes necessary and there could be no success for an orchestra in which individual musicians played according to their own fancy and refused to follow the indications of the conductor. In spiritual things also the same rule holds; a sadhak who disregarded the guidance of the Guru and preferred the untrained inspirations of the novice could hardly escape the stumbles or even the disasters which so often lie thick around the path to spiritual realisation. I need not enumerate the other benefits which can be drawn from the training that sport can give or dwell on their use in the national life; what I have said is sufficient. At any rate, in schools like ours and in universities sports have now a recognised and indispensable place; for even a highest and completest education of the mind is not enough without the education of the body. Where the qualities I have enumerated are absent or insufficiently present, a strong individual will or a national will may build them up, but the aid given by sports to their development is direct and in no way negligible. This would be a sufficient reason for the attention given to them in our Ashram, though there are others which I need not mention here. I am concerned here with their importance and the necessity of the qualities they create or stimulate for our national life. The nation which possesses them in the highest degree is likely to be the strongest for victory, success and greatness, but also for the contribution it can make towards the bringing about of unity and a more harmonious world order towards which we look as our hope for humanity's future.

December 30, 1948

PERFECTION OF THE BODY

The perfection of the body, as great a perfection as we can bring about by the means at our disposal, must be the ultimate aim of physical culture. Perfection is the true aim of all culture, the spiritual and psychic, the mental, the vital and it must be the aim of our physical culture also. If our seeking is for a total perfection of the being, the physical part of it cannot be left aside; for the body is the material basis, the body is the instrument which we have to use. *Śarīram khalu dharmasādhanam*, says the old Sanskrit adage, — the body is the means of fulfilment of dharma, and dharma means every ideal which we can propose to ourselves and the law of its working out and its action. A total perfection is the ultimate aim which we set before us, for our ideal is the Divine Life which we wish to create here, the life of the Spirit fulfilled on earth, life accomplishing its own spiritual transformation even here on earth in the conditions of the material universe. That cannot be unless the body too undergoes a transformation, unless its action and functioning attain to a supreme capacity and the perfection which is possible to it or which can be made possible.

I have already indicated in a previous message a relative perfection of the physical consciousness in the body and of the mind, the life, the character which it houses as, no less than an awakening and development of the body's own native capacities, a desirable outcome of the exercises and practices of the physical culture to which we have commenced to give in this Ashram a special attention and scope. A development of the physical consciousness must always be a considerable part of our aim, but for that the right development of the body itself is an essential element; health, strength, fitness are the first needs, but the physical frame itself must be the best possible. A divine life in a material world implies necessarily a union of the two ends of existence, the spiritual summit and the material base. The soul with the basis of its life established in Matter ascends to the heights of the Spirit but does not cast away its base, it joins the heights and the depths together. The Spirit descends into Matter and the material world with all its lights and glories and powers and with them fills and transforms life in the material world so that it becomes more and more divine. The transformation is not a change into something purely subtle and spiritual to which Matter is in its nature repugnant and by which it is felt as an obstacle or as a shackle binding the Spirit; it takes up Matter as a form of the Spirit though now a form which conceals and turns it into a revealing instrument, it does not cast away the energies of Matter, its capacities, its methods; it brings out their hidden possibilities, uplifts, sublimates, discloses their innate divinity. The divine life will reject nothing that is capable of divinisation; all is to be seized, exalted, made utterly perfect. The mind now still ignorant, though struggling towards knowledge, has to rise towards and into the supramental light and truth and bring it down so that it shall suffuse our thinking and perception and insight and all our means of knowing till they become radiant with the highest truth in their inmost and outermost movements. Our life, still full of obscurity and confusion and occupied with so many dull and lower aims, must feel all its urges and instincts exalted and irradiated and become a glorious counterpart of the supramental super-life above. The physical consciousness and physical being, the body itself must reach a perfection in all that it is and does which now we can hardly conceive. It may even in the end be suffused with a light and beauty and bliss from the Beyond and the life divine assume a body divine.

But first the evolution of the nature must have reached a point at which it can meet the Spirit direct, feel the aspiration towards the spiritual change and open itself to the workings of the Power which shall transform it. A supreme perfection, a total perfection is possible only by a transformation of our lower or human nature, a transformation of the mind into a thing of light, our life into a thing of power, an instrument of right action, right use for all its forces, of a happy elevation of its being lifting it beyond its present comparatively narrow potentiality for a self-fulfilling force of action and joy of life. There must be equally a transforming change of the body by a conversion of its action, its functioning, its capacities as an instrument beyond the limitations by which it is clogged and hampered even in its greatest present human attainment. In the totality of the change we have to achieve, human means and forces too have to be taken up, not dropped but used and magnified to their utmost possibility as part of the new life. Such a sublimation of our present human powers of mind and life into elements of a divine life on earth can be conceived without much difficulty; but in what figure shall we conceive the perfection of the body?

In the past the body has been regarded by spiritual seekers rather as an obstacle, as something to be overcome and discarded than as an instrument of spiritual perfection and a field of the spiritual change. It has been condemned as a grossness of Matter, as an insuperable impediment and the limitations of the body as something unchangeable making transformation impossible. This is because the human body even at its best seems only to be driven by an energy of life which has its own limits and is debased in its smaller physical activities by much that is petty or coarse or evil, the body in itself is burdened with the inertia and inconscience of Matter, only partly awake and, although quickened and animated by a nervous activity, subconscient in the fundamental action of its constituent cells and tissues and their secret workings. Even in its fullest strength and force and greatest glory of beauty, it is still a flower of the material Inconscience; the inconscient is the soil from which it has grown and at every point opposes a narrow boundary to the extension of its powers and to any effort of radical self-exceeding. But if a divine life is possible on earth, then this self-exceeding must also be possible.

In the pursuit of perfection we can start at either end of our range of being and we have then to use, initially at least, the means and processes proper to our choice. In Yoga the process is spiritual and psychic; even its vital and physical processes are given a spiritual or psychic turn and raised to a higher motion than belongs properly to the ordinary life and Matter, as for instance in the Hathayogic and Rajayogic use of the breathing or the use of Asana. Ordinarily a previous preparation of the mind and life and body is necessary to make them fit for the reception of the spiritual energy and the organisation of psychic forces and methods, but this too is given a special turn proper to the Yoga. On the other hand, if we start in any field at the lower end we have to employ the means and processes which Life and Matter offer to us and respect the conditions and what we may call the technique imposed by the vital and the material energy. We may extend the activity, the achievement, the perfection attained beyond the initial, even beyond the normal possibilities but still we have to stand on the same base with which we started and within the boundaries it gives to us. It is not that the action from the two ends cannot meet and the higher take into itself and uplift the lower perfection; but this can usually be done only by a transition from the lower to a higher outlook, aspiration and motive: this we shall have to do if our aim is to transform the human into the divine life. But here there comes in the necessity of taking up the activities of human life and sublimating them by the power of the spirit. Here the lower perfection will not disappear; it will remain but will be enlarged and transformed by the higher perfection which only the power of the spirit can give. This will be evident if we consider poetry and art, philosophic thought, the perfection of the written word or the perfect organisation of earthly life: these have to be taken up and the possibilities already achieved or whatever perfection has already been attained included in a new and greater perfection but with the larger vision and inspiration of a spiritual consciousness and with new forms and powers. It must be the same with the perfection of the body.

The taking up of life and Matter into what is essentially a spiritual seeking, instead of the rejection and ultimate exclusion of them which was the attitude of a spirituality that shunned or turned away from life in the world, involves certain developments which a spiritual institution of the older kind could regard as foreign to its purpose. A divine life in the world or an institution having that for its aim and purpose cannot be or cannot remain something outside or entirely shut away from the life of ordinary men in the world or unconcerned with the mundane existence; it has to do

the work of the Divine in the world and not a work outside
or separate from it. The life of the ancient Rishis in their
Ashramas had such a connection; they were creators, edu-
cators, guides of men and the life of the Indian people in
ancient times was largely developed and directed by their
shaping influence. The life and activities involved in the new
endeavour are not identical but they too must be an action
upon the world and a new creation in it. It must have con-
tacts and connections with it and activities which take their
place in the general life and whose initial or primary objects
may not seem to differ from those of the same activities in
the outside world. In our Ashram here we have found it
necessary to establish a school for the education of the
children of the resident Sadhaks teaching upon familiar lines
though with certain modifications and taking as part and an
important part of their development an intensive physical
training which has given form to the sports and athletics
practised by the Jeunesse Sportive of the Ashram and of
which this Bulletin is the expression. It has been questioned
by some what place sports can have in an Ashram created
for spiritual seekers and what connection there can be
between spirituality and sports. The first answer lies in what
I have already written about the connections of an institution of this kind with the activities of the general life of men
and what I have indicated in the previous number as to the
utility such a training can have for the life of a nation and
its benefit for the international life. Another answer can
occur to us if we look beyond first objects and turn to the
aspiration for a total perfection including the perfection
of the body.

In the admission of an activity such as sports and physical
exercises into the life of the Ashram it is evident that the

methods and the first objects to be attained must belong to what we have called the lower end of the being. Originally they have been introduced for the physical education and bodily development of the children of the Ashram School and these are too young for a strictly spiritual aim or practice to enter into their activities and it is not certain that any great number of them will enter the spiritual life when they are of an age to choose what shall be the direction of their future. The object must be the training of the body and the development of certain parts of mind and character so far as this can be done by or in connection with this training and I have already indicated in a previous number how and in what directions this can be done. It is a relative and human perfection that can be attained within these limits; anything greater can be reached only by the intervention of higher powers, psychic powers, the power of the spirit. Yet what can be attained within the human boundaries can be something very considerable and sometimes immense: what we call genius is part of the development of the human range of being and its achievements, especially in things of the mind and will, can carry us halfway to the divine. Even what the mind and will can do with the body in the field proper to the body and its life, in the way of physical achievement, bodily endurance, feats of prowess of all kinds, a lasting activity refusing fatigue or collapse and continuing beyond what seems at first to be possible, courage and refusal to succumb under an endless and murderous physical suffering, these and other victories of many kinds sometimes approaching or reaching the miraculous are seen in the human field and must be reckoned as a part of our concept of a total perfection. The unflinching and persistent reply that can be made by the body as well as the mind of man and by his life-energy to whatever call can be imposed on it in the most difficult and discouraging circumstances by the necessities of war and travel and adventure is of the same kind and their endurance can reach astounding proportions and even the inconscient in the body seems to be able to return a surprising response.

The body, we have said, is a creation of the Inconscient and itself inconscient or at least subconscient in parts of its self and much of its hidden action; but what we call the Inconscient is an appearance, a dwelling place, an instrument of a secret Consciousness or a Superconscient which has created the miracle we call the universe. Matter is the field and the creation of the Inconscient and the perfection of the operations of inconscient Matter, their perfect adaptation of means to an aim and end, the wonders they perform and the marvels of beauty they create, testify, in spite of all the ignorant denial we can oppose, to the presence and power of consciousness of this Superconscience in every part and movement of the material universe. It is there in the body, has made it and its emergence in our consciousness is the secret aim of evolution and the key to the mystery of our existence.

In the use of such activities as sports and physical exercises for the education of the individual in childhood and first youth, which should mean the bringing out of his actual and latent possibilities to their fullest development, the means and methods we must use are limited by the nature of the body and its aim must be such relative human perfection of the body's powers and capacities and those of the powers of mind, will, character, action of which it is at once the residence and the instrument so far as these methods can help to develop them. I have written sufficiently about the mental and moral parts of perfection to which these pursuits can contribute and this I need not repeat here. For the body itself the perfections that can be developed by these means are those of its natural qualities and capacities and, secondly, the training of its general fitness, as an instrument for all the activities which may be demanded from it by the mind and the will, by the life-energy or by the dynamic perceptions, impulses and instincts of our subtle physical being which is an unrecognised but very important element and agent in our nature. Health and strength are the first conditions for the natural perfection of the body, not only muscular strength and the solid strength of the limbs and physical stamina, but the finer, alert and plastic and adaptable force which our nervous and subtle physical parts can put into the activities of the frame. There is also the still more dynamic force which a call upon the life-energies can bring into the body and stir it to greater activities, even feats of the most extraordinary character of which in its normal state it would not be capable. There is also the strength which the mind and will by their demands and stimulus and by their secret powers which we use or by which we are used without knowing clearly the source of their action can impart to the body or impose upon it as masters and inspirers. Among the natural qualities and powers of the body which can be thus awakened, stimulated and trained to a normal activity we must reckon dexterity and stability in all kinds of physical action such as swiftness in the race, dexterity in combat, skill and endurance of the mountaineer, the constant and often extraordinary response to all that can be demanded from the body of the soldier, sailor, traveller or explorer to which I have already made reference or in adventure of all kinds and all the wide range of physical attainment to

which man has accustomed himself or to which he is exceptionally pushed by his own will or by the compulsion of cir-
cumstance. It is a general fitness of the body for all that can
be asked from it which is the common formula of all this
action, a fitness attained by a few or by many, that could
be generalised by an extended and many-sided physical
education and discipline. Some of these activities can be
included under the name of sports; there are others for
which sport and physical exercises can be an effective preparation. In some of them a training for common action,
combined movement, discipline are needed and for that our
physical exercises can make one ready; in others a developed
individual will, skill of mind and quick perception, forceful-
ness of life-energy and subtle physical impulsion are more
prominently needed and may even be the one sufficient
trainer. All must be included in our conception of the
natural powers of the body and its capacity and instrumental fitness in the service of the human mind and will
and therefore in our concept of the total perfection of the
body.

There are two conditions for this perfection, an awakening
in as great an entirety as possible of the body consciousness
and an education, an evocation of its potentialities, also
as entire and fully developed and, it may be, as many-sided
as possible. The form or body is, no doubt, in its origin a
creation of the Inconscient and limited by it on all sides,
but still of the Inconscient developing the secret consciousness concealed within it and growing in light of knowledge,
power and Ananda. We have to take it at the point it has
reached in its human evolution in these things, make as full
a use of them as may be and, as much as we can, further this
evolution to as high a degree as is permitted by the force

of the individual temperament and nature. In all forms in the world there is a force at work, unconsciously active or oppressed by inertia in its lower formulations, but in the human being conscious from the first, with its potentialities partly awake, partly asleep or latent: what is awake in it we have to make fully conscious; what is asleep we have to arouse and set to its work; what is latent we have to evoke and educate. Here there are two aspects of the body consciousness, one which seems to be a kind of automatism carrying on its work in the physical plane without any intervention of the mind and in parts even beyond any possibility of direct observation by the mind or, if conscious or observable, still proceeding or capable of continuing, when once started, by an apparently mechanical action not needing direction by the mind and continuing so long as the mind does not intervene.

There are other movements taught and trained by the mind which can yet go on operating automatically but faultlessly even when not attended to by the thought or will; there are others which can operate in sleep and produce results of value to the waking intelligence. But more important is what may be described as a trained and developed automatism, a perfected skill and capacity of eye and ear and the hands and all the members prompt to respond to any call made on them, a developed spontaneous operation as an instrument, a complete fitness for any demand that the mind and life-energy can make upon it. This is ordinarily the best we can achieve at the lower end, when we start from that end and limit ourselves to the means and methods which are proper to it. For more we have to turn to the mind and life-energy themselves or to the energy of the spirit and to what they can do for a greater perfection

of the body. The most we can do in the physical field by
physical means is necessarily insecure as well as bound
by limits; even what seems a perfect health and strength of
the body is precarious and can be broken down at any
moment by fluctuations from within or by a strong attack
or shock from outside: only by the breaking of our limitations can a higher and more enduring perfection come. One
direction in which our consciousness must grow is an increasing hold from within or from above on the body and its
powers and its more conscious response to the higher parts
of our being. The mind pre-eminently is man; he is a mental
being and his human perfection grows the more he fulfils
the description of the Upanishad, a mental being, Purusha,
leader of the life and the body. If the mind can take up and
control the instincts and automatisms of the life-energy
and the subtle physical consciousness and the body, if it
can enter into them, consciously use and, as we may say,
fully mentalise their instinctive or spontaneous action, the
perfection of these energies, their action too becomes more
conscious and more aware of itself and more perfect. But
it is necessary for the mind too to grow in perfection and
this it can do best when it depends less on the fallible
intellect of physical mind, when it is not limited even by the
more orderly and accurate working of the reason and can
grow in intuition and acquire a wider, deeper and closer
seeing and the more luminous drive of energy of a higher
intuitive will. Even within the limits of its present evolution
it is difficult to measure the degree to which the mind is able
to extend its control or its use of the body's powers and capacities and when the mind rises to higher powers still and
pushes back its human boundaries, it becomes impossible
to fix any limits: even, in certain realisations, an interven-

tion by the will in the automatic working of the bodily organs seems to become possible. Wherever limitations recede and in proportion as they recede, the body becomes a more plastic and responsive and in that measure a more fit and perfect instrument of the action of the spirit. In all effective and expressive activities here in the material world the cooperation of the two ends of our being is indispensable. If the body is unable whether by fatigue or by natural incapacity or any other cause to second the thought or will or is in any way irresponsive or insufficiently responsive, to that extent the action fails or falls short or becomes in some degree unsatisfying or incomplete. In what seems to be an exploit of the spirit so purely mental as the outpouring of poetic inspiration, there must be a responsive vibration of the brain and its openness as a channel for the power of the thought and vision and the light of the word that is making or breaking its way through or seeking for its perfect expression. If the brain is fatigued or dulled by any clog, either the inspiration cannot come and nothing is written or it fails and something inferior is all that can come out; or else a lower inspiration takes the place of the more luminous formulation that was striving to shape itself or the brain finds it more easy to lend itself to a less radiant stimulus or else it labours and constructs or responds to poetic artifice. Even in the most purely mental activities the fitness, readiness or perfect training of the bodily instrument is a condition indispensable. That readiness, that response too is part of the total perfection of the body.

The essential purpose and sign of the growing evolution here is the emergence of consciousness in an apparently inconscient universe, the growth of the consciousness and with it growth of the light and power of the being; the development of the form and its functioning or its fitness to survive, although indispensable, is not the whole meaning or the central motive. The greater and greater awakening of consciousness and its climb to a higher and higher level and a wider extent of its vision and action is the condition of our progress towards that supreme and total perfection which is the aim of our existence. It is the condition also of the total perfection of the body. There are higher levels of the mind than any we now conceive and to these we must one day reach and rise beyond them to the heights of a greater, a spiritual existence. As we rise we have to open to them our lower members and fill these with those superior and supreme dynamisms of light and power; the body we have to make a more and more and even entirely conscious frame and instrument, a conscious sign and seal and power of the spirit. As it grows in this perfection, the force and extent of its dynamic action and its response and service to the spirit must increase, the control of the spirit over it also must grow and the plasticity of its functioning both in its developed and acquired parts of power and in its automatic responses down to those that are now purely organic and seem to be the movements of a mechanic inconscience. This cannot happen without a veritable transformation and a transformation of the mind and life and very body is indeed the change to which our evolution is secretly moving and without this transformation the entire fullness of a divine life on earth cannot emerge. In this transformation the body itself can become an agent and a partner. It might indeed be possible for the spirit to achieve a considerable manifestation with only a passive and imperfectly conscious body as its last or bottommost means of material functioning, but this could not be anything perfect or complete. A fully conscious body might even discover and work out the right material method and process of a material transformation. For this, no doubt, the spirit's supreme light and power and creative joy must have manifested on the summit of the individual consciousness and sent down their fiat into the body, but still the body may take in the working out its spontaneous part of self-discovery and achievement. It would be thus a participator and agent in its own transformation and the integral transformation of the whole being; this too would be a part and a sign and evidence of the total perfection of the body.

If the emergence and growth of consciousness is the central motive of the evolution and the key to its secret purpose, then by the very nature of that evolution this growth must involve not only a wider and wider extent of its capacities but also an ascent to a higher and higher level till it reaches the highest possible. For it starts from a nethermost level of involution in the Inconscience which we see at work in Matter creating the material universe; it proceeds by an Ignorance which is yet ever developing knowledge and reaching out to an ever greater light and ever greater organisation and efficacy of the will and harmonisation of all its own inherent and emerging powers; it must at last reach a point where it develops or acquires the complete fullness of its capacity and that must be a state or action in which there is no longer an ignorance seeking for knowledge but Knowledge self-possessed, inherent in the being, master of its own truths and working them out with a natural vision and force that is not afflicted by limitation or error. Or if there is a limitation, it must be a self-imposed veil behind which it would keep truth back for a manifestation in Time but draw it out at will and without any need of search or acquisition in the order of a right perception of things or in the just succession of that which has to be manifested in obedience to the call of Time. This would mean an entry or approach into what might be called a truth-consciousness self-existent in which the being would be aware of its own realities and would have the inherent power to manifest them in a Time-creation in which all would be Truth following out its own unerring steps and combining its own harmonies; every thought and will and feeling and act would be spontaneously right, inspired or intuitive, moving by the light of Truth and therefore perfect. All would express inherent realities of the spirit; some fullness of the power of the spirit would be there. One would have overpassed the present limitations of mind: mind would become a seeing of the light of Truth, will a force and power of the Truth, Life a progressive fulfilment of the Truth, the body itself a conscious vessel of the Truth and part of the means of its self-effectuation and a form of its self-aware existence. It would be at least some initiation of this Truth-Consciousness, some first figure and action of it that must be reached and enter into a first operation if there is to be a divine life or any full manifestation of a spiritualised consciousness in the world of Matter. Or, at the very least, such a Truth-Consciousness must be in communication with our own mind and life and body, descend into touch with it, control its seeing and action, impel its motives, take hold of its forces and shape their direction and purpose. All touched by it might not be able to embody it fully, but each would give some form to it according to his spiritual temperament, inner capacity, the line of his evolution in Nature: he would reach securely the perfection of which he was immediately capable and he would be on the road to the full possession of the truth of the Spirit and of the truth of Nature.

In the workings of such a Truth-Consciousness there would be a certain conscious seeing and willing automatism of the steps of its truth which would replace the infallible automatism of the inconscient or seemingly inconscient Force that has brought out of an apparent Void the miracle of an ordered universe and this could create a new order of the manifestation of the being in which a perfect perfection would become possible, even a supreme and total perfection would appear in the vistas of an ultimate possibility. If we could draw down this power into the material world, our agelong dreams of human perfectibility, individual perfection, the perfectibility of the race, of society, inner mastery over self and a complete mastery, governance and utilisation of the forces of Nature could see at long last a prospect of total achievement. This complete human self-fulfilment might well pass beyond limitations and be transformed into the character of a divine life. Matter after taking into itself and manifesting the power of life and the light of mind would draw down into it the superior or supreme power and light of the spirit and in an earthly body shed its parts of inconscience and become a perfectly conscious frame of the spirit. A secure completeness and stability of the health and strength of its physical tenement could be maintained by the will and force of this inhabitant; all the natural capacities of the physical frame, all powers of the physical consciousness would reach their utmost extension and be there at command and sure of their flawless action. As an instrument the body would acquire a fullness of capacity, a totality of fitness for all uses which the inhabitant would demand of it far beyond anything now possible. Even it could become a revealing vessel of a supreme beauty and bliss, — casting the beauty of the light of the spirit suffusing and radiating from it as a lamp reflects and diffuses the luminosity of its indwelling flame, carrying in itself the beatitude of the spirit, its joy of the seeing mind, its joy of life and spiritual happiness, the joy of Matter released into a spiritual consciousness and thrilled with a constant ecstasy. This would be the total perfection of the spiritualised body.

All this might not come all at once, though such a sudden illumination might be possible if a divine Power and Light and Ananda could take their stand on the summit of our being and send down their force into the mind and life and body illumining and remoulding the cells, awaking consciousness in all the frame. But the way would be open and the consummation of all that is possible in the individual could progressively take place. The physical also would have its share in that consummation of the whole.

There would always remain vistas beyond as the infinite Spirit took up towards higher heights and larger breadths the evolving Nature, in the movement of the liberated being towards the possession of the supreme Reality, the supreme existence, consciousness, beatitude. But of this it would be premature to speak: what has been written is perhaps as much as the human mind as it is now constituted can venture to look forward to and the enlightened thought understand in some measure. These consequences of the Truth-Consciousness descending and laying its hold upon Matter would be a sufficient justification of the evolutionary labour. In this upward all-uplifting sweep of the Spirit there could be a simultaneous or consecutive downward sweep of the triumph of a spiritualised Nature all-including, all-transmuting and in it there could occur a glorifying change of Matter and the physical consciousness and physical form and functioning of which we could speak as not only the total but the supreme perfection of the body.

THE MOTHER ON EDUCATION

The Mother's original writings in French of which the translations are reproduced here, were, all except "To the Children of the Ashram", first printed in the bilingual quarterly, the *Bulletin of Physical Education*, later called the *Bulletin of Sri Aurobindo International Centre of Education*.

On Education*

I

THE SCIENCE OF LIVING

(To Know Oneself and Control Oneself)

An aimless life is always a miserable life.

Everyone of you should have an aim. But do not forget that on the quality of your aim will depend the quality of your life.

Your aim should be high and wide, generous and disinterested; this will make your life precious to yourself and to others.

But whatever your ideal, it cannot be perfectly realised unless you have realised perfection in yourself.

To work for your perfection the first step is to become conscious of yourself, of the different parts of your being and their respective activities. You must learn to distinguish these different parts one from the other, so that you may find out clearly the origin of the movements that occur in you, the many impulses, reactions and conflicting wills that drive you to action. It is an assiduous study which demands much perseverance and sincerity. For man's nature, specially his mental nature, has a spontaneous tendency to give a favourable explanation for whatever he thinks, feels,

* First published in the *Bulletin of Physical Education*, Sri Aurobindo Ashram, Pondicherry, from Nov. 1950 to Feb. 1952. Printed also in book form as: *The Mother on Education*, Sri Aurobindo Ashram, Pondicherry, 1952.

says and does. It is only by observing these movements with great care, by bringing them, as it were, before the tribunal of our highest ideal, with a sincere will to submit to its judgment, that we can hope to educate in us a discernment which does not err. For if we truly want to progress and acquire the capacity of knowing the truth of our being, that is to say, the one thing for which we have been really created, that which we can call our mission upon earth, then we must, in a very regular and constant manner, reject from us or eliminate in us whatever contradicts the truth of our existence, whatever is in opposition to it. It is thus that little by little all the parts, all the elements of our being, could be organised into a homogeneous whole around our psychic centre. This work of unification demands a long time to be brought to some degree of perfection. Hence, to accomplish it, we must arm ourselves with patience and endurance, with a determination to prolong our life as far as it is necessary for the success of our endeavour.

As we pursue this labour of purification and unification, we must at the same time take great care to perfect the external and instrumental part of our being. When the higher truth will manifest, it must find in you a mental being supple and rich enough to be able to give to the idea seeking to express itself a form of thought which preserves its force and clarity. This thought, again, when it seeks to clothe itself in words must find in you a sufficient power of expression so that the words reveal the thought and not deform it. And this formula in which you embody the truth should be made articulate in all your sentiments, all your willings and acts, all the movements of your being. Finally, these movements themselves should, by constant effort, attain their highest perfection.

All this can be realised by means of a fourfold discipline the general outline of which is given here. These four aspects of the discipline do not exclude each other, and can be followed at the same time, indeed it is better to do so. The starting-point is what can be called the psychic discipline. We give the name 'psychic' to the psychological centre of our being, the seat within of the highest truth of our existence, that which can know and manifest this truth. It is therefore of capital importance for us to become conscious of its presence within us, to concentrate on this presence and make it a living fact for us and identify ourselves with it.

Through space and time many methods have been framed to attain this perception and finally to achieve this identification. Some methods are psychological, some religious, some even mechanical. In reality, everyone has to find out that which suits him best, and if one has a sincere and steady aspiration, a persistent and dynamic will, one is sure to meet in one way or another, externally by study and instruction, internally by concentration, meditation, revelation and experience, the help one needs to reach the goal. Only one thing is absolutely indispensable: the will to discover and realise. This discovery and this realisation should be the primary occupation of the being, the pearl of great price which one should acquire at any cost. Whatever you do, whatever your occupation and activity, the will to find the truth of your being and to unite with it must always be living, always present behind all that you do, all that you experience, all that you think.

To complete this movement of inner discovery, it is good not to neglect the mental development. For the mental instrument can be equally a great help or a great hindrance. In its natural state the human mind is always limited in its vision, narrow in its understanding, rigid in its conceptions, and a certain effort is needed to enlarge it, make it supple and deep. Hence, it is very necessary that one should consider everything from as many points of view as possible. There is an exercise in this connection which gives great suppleness and elevation to thought. It is as follows. A clearly formulated thesis is set; against it is opposed the antithesis, formulated with the same precision. Then by careful reflection the problem must be widened or transcended so that a synthesis is found which unites the two contraries in a larger, higher and more comprehensive idea.

Many exercises of the same kind can be undertaken; some have a beneficial effect on the character and so possess a double advantage, that of educating the mind and that of establishing control over one's feelings and their results. For example, you must never allow your mind to judge things and people; for the mind is not an instrument of knowledge — it is incapable of finding knowledge — but it must be moved by knowledge. Knowledge belongs to a region much higher than that of the human mind, even beyond the region of pure ideas. The mind has to be made silent and attentive in order to receive knowledge from above and manifest it. For it is an instrument of formation, organisation and action. And it is in these functions that it attains its full value and real utility.

Another practice may be very helpful for the progress of the consciousness. Whenever there is a disagreement on any matter, such as a decision to take, or an act to accomplish, one must not stick to one's own conception or point of view. On the contrary, one must try to understand the other's point of view, put oneself in his place and, instead of quarrelling or even fighting, find out a solution which can reasonably satisfy both parties; there is always one for men of goodwill.

Here must be mentioned the training of the vital. The vital being in us is the seat of impulses and desires, of enthusiasm and violence, of dynamic energy and desperate depression, of passions and revolt. It can set in motion everything, build up and realise, it can also destroy and mar everything. It seems to be, in the human being, the most difficult part to train. It is a long labour requiring great patience, and it demands a perfect sincerity, for without sincerity one will deceive oneself from the very first step, and all endeavour for progress will go in vain. With the collaboration of the vital no realisation seems impossible, no transformation impracticable. But the difficulty lies in securing this constant collaboration. The vital is a good worker, but most often it seeks its own satisfaction. If that is refused, totally or even partially, it gets vexed, sulky and goes on strike; the energy disappears more or less completely and leaves in its place disgust for people and things, discouragement or revolt, depression and dissatisfaction. At these moments one must remain quiet and refuse to act; for it is at such times that one does stupid things and in a few minutes can destroy or spoil what one has gained in months of regular effort, losing thus all the progress made. These crises are of less duration and are less dangerous in the case of those who have established a contact with their psychic being sufficient to keep alive in them the flame of aspiration and the consciousness of the ideal to be realised. They can, with the help of this consciousness, deal with their vital as one deals with a child in revolt, with patience and perseverance showing it the truth and light, endeavouring to convince it and awaken in it the goodwill which for a moment was veiled. With the help of such patient intervention each crisis can be changed into a new progress, into a further step towards the goal. Progress may be slow, falls may be frequent, but if a courageous will is maintained one is sure to triumph one day and see all difficulties melt and vanish before the radiant consciousness of truth.

Lastly, we must, by means of a rational and clear-seeing physical education, make our body strong and supple so that it may become in the material world a fit instrument for the truth-force which wills to manifest through us.

In fact, the body must not rule, it has to obey. By its very nature it is a docile and faithful servant. Unfortunately it has not often the capacity of discernment with regard to its masters, the mind and the vital. It obeys them blindly, at the cost of its own well-being. The mind with its dogmas, its rigid and arbitrary principles, the vital with its passions, its excesses and dissipations soon do everything to destroy the natural balance of the body and create in it fatigue, exhaustion and disease. It must be freed from this tyranny; that can be done only through a constant union with the psychic centre of the being. The body has a wonderful capacity of adaptation and endurance. It is fit to do so many more things than one can usually imagine. If instead of the ignorant and despotic masters that govern it, it is ruled by the central truth of the being, one will be surprised at what it is capable of doing. Calm and quiet, strong and poised, it will at every minute put forth effort that is demanded of it, for it will have learnt to find rest in action, to recuperate through contact with the universal forces the energies it spends consciously and usefully. In this sound and balanced life a new harmony will manifest in the body, reflecting the harmony of the higher regions which will give it the perfect proportions and the ideal beauty of form. And this harmony will be progressive, for the truth of the being is never static, it is a continual unfolding of a growing, a more and more global and comprehensive perfection. As soon as the body learns to follow the movement of a progressive harmony, it will be possible for it, through a continuous process of transformation, to escape the necessity of disintegration and destruction. Thus the irrevocable law of death will have no reason for existing any more.

As we rise to this degree of perfection which is our goal, we shall perceive that the truth we seek is made up of four major aspects: Love, Knowledge, Power and Beauty. These four attributes of the Truth will spontaneously express themselves in our being. The psychic will be the vehicle of true and pure love, the mind that of infallible knowledge, the vital will manifest an invincible power and strength and the body will be the expression of a perfect beauty and a perfect harmony.

II

EDUCATION

The education of a human being should begin at his very birth and continue throughout his life.

Indeed, if the education is to have its maximum result, it must begin even before birth: it is the mother herself who proceeds with this education by means of a twofold action, first, upon herself for her own improvement, and secondly, upon the child which she is forming within her physically. For it is certain that the nature of the child about to be born will depend very much upon the mother who forms it, upon her aspiration and will as much as upon the material surroundings in which she lives. The part of education which the mother has to go through is to see that her thoughts are always beautiful and pure, her feelings always noble and fine, her material surroundings as harmonious as possible and full of a great simplicity. And if in addition she has a conscious and definite will to form the child according to the highest ideal she can conceive, then the very best conditions are provided for the child to come into the world with the maximum of possibilities. How many difficult efforts and useless complications are avoided thereby!

Education to be complete must have five principal aspects relating to the five principal activities of the human being: the physical, the vital, the mental, the psychic and the spiritual. Usually, these phases of education succeed each other in a chronological order following the growth of the individual; this, however, does not mean that the one should replace the other but that all must continue, completing each other, till the end of life.

We propose to study these five aspects of education one by one and also their reciprocal relations. But before we enter into the details of the subject, I wish to make a recommendation to parents. The majority of them, for various reasons, take very little thought of a true education to be given to children. When they have brought a child into the world, and when they have given him food and satisfied his various material wants by looking more or less carefully to the maintenance of his health, they think they have fully discharged their duty. Later on, they would put him to school and hand over to the teacher the care of his education.

There are other parents who know that their children should receive education and try to give it. But very few among them, even among those who are most serious and sincere, know that the first thing to do, in order to be able to educate the child, is to educate oneself, to become conscious and master of oneself so that one does not set a bad example to one's child. For it is through example that education becomes effective. To say good words, give wise advice to a child has very little effect, if one does not show by one's living example the truth of what one teaches. Sincerity, honesty, straightforwardness, courage, disinterestedness, unselfishness, patience, endurance, perseverance, peace, calm, self-control are all things that are taught infinitely better by example than by beautiful speeches. Parents, you should have a high ideal and act always in accordance with that ideal. You will see little by little your child reflecting this ideal in himself and manifesting spontaneously the qualities you wish to see expressed in his nature. Quite naturally a child has respect and admiration for his parents;

unless they are quite unworthy, they will appear always to their children as demigods whom they will seek to imitate as well as they can.

With very few exceptions, parents do not take into account the disastrous influence their defects, impulses, weaknesses, want of self-control have on their children. If you wish to be respected by your child, have respect for yourself and be at every moment worthy of respect. Never be arbitrary, despotic, impatient, ill-tempered. When your child asks you a question, do not answer him by a stupidity or a foolishness, under the pretext that he cannot understand you. You can always make yourself understood if you take sufficient pains for it, and in spite of the popular saying that it is not always good to tell the truth, I affirm that it is always good to tell the truth, only the art consists in telling it in such a way as to make it accessible to the brain of the hearer. In early life, till he is twelve or fourteen, the child's mind is hardly accessible to abstract notions and general ideas. And yet you can train it to understand these things by using concrete images or symbols or parables. Up to a sufficiently advanced age and for some who mentally remain always children, a narrative, a story, a tale told well teaches much more than a heap of theoretical explanations.

Another pitfall to avoid: do not scold your child except with a definite purpose and only when quite indispensable. A child too often scolded gets hardened to rebuke and no longer attaches much importance to words or severity of tone. Particularly, take care not to rebuke him for a fault which you yourself commit. Children are very keen and clear-sighted observers: they soon find out your weaknesses and note them without pity.

When a child has made a mistake, see that he confesses

it to you spontaneously and frankly; and when he has confessed, make him understand with kindness and affection
what was wrong in his movement and that he should not
repeat it. In any case, never scold him; a fault confessed
must be forgiven. You should not allow any fear to slip in
between you and your child; fear is a disastrous way to education: invariably it gives birth to dissimulation and falsehood. Only an affection that is discerning, firm yet gentle
and a sufficient practical knowledge will create bonds of
trust that are indispensable for you to make the education
of your child effective. And never forget that you have to
surmount yourself always and constantly so as to be at the
height of your task and truly fulfil the duty which you owe
your child by the mere fact of your having brought him
into existence.

III

PHYSICAL EDUCATION

Of all the domains of human consciousness, the physical is the one most completely governed by method, order, discipline, procedure. The lack of plasticity and receptivity in matter has to be replaced there by an organisation of details, at once precise and comprehensive. In this organisation one must not forget, however, that all the domains of the being are interdependent and interpenetrating. Yet, even if a mental or vital impulsion is to be expressed physically it must submit to an exact and precise procedure. That is why all education of the body, if it is to be effective, must be rigorous and detailed, foreseeing and methodical. That will be translated into habits: the body is a being of habits. But these should be controlled and disciplined, yet at the same time supple enough to adapt themselves to the circumstances and the needs of the growth and development of the being.

All education of the body should begin at the very birth and continue throughout life: it is never too soon to begin nor too late to continue.

The education of the body has three principal aspects: (1) control and discipline of functions, (2) a total, methodical and harmonious development of all the parts and movements of the body and (3) rectification of defects and deformities, if there are any.

It may be said that from the very first days, almost even from the first hours, of his life the child should undergo the first part of the programme in the matter of food, sleep, evacuation, etc. If the child, from the very beginning of his existence, takes to good habits, that will save him a good deal of trouble and inconvenience all the rest of his life. And also those who have the charge to watch over him during his first years will find their task very much easier.

Naturally, this education, if it is to be rational, enlightened and effective, must be based upon a minimum knowledge of the human body, its structure and its functions. As the child grows, he must gradually acquire the habit of observing the functioning of his organs so that he may control them more and more, taking care that this functioning is normal and harmonious. In the matter of positions, postures and movements, bad habits are formed too early and too quickly that may have disastrous consequences for the whole life. Those who take the question of education seriously and wish to give their children all facilities to develop normally will easily find the necessary hints and instructions. The subject is being more and more carefully studied, and many books have appeared and are appearing which give all the information and guidance needed on the subject.

It is not possible for me to enter into details of the execution, for each problem is different from another and the solution should suit the individual case. The question of food has been studied by experts at length and with care; the dietary to help children in their growth is generally known and can be usefully followed. But it is very important to remember that the instinct of the body, so long as it remains intact, knows more than any theory. Thus, if you wish that your children should develop normally, you must not force them to eat food for which they have a disgust; for often the body possesses a sure instinct as to what is harmful to it, unless the child is particularly capricious.

The body in its normal state, that is to say, if there is no intervention of mental notions or vital impulsions, knows also very well what is good and necessary for it; but this can happen effectively when the child has been taught with care and has learnt to distinguish desires from needs. He must develop a taste for food that is simple and healthy, substantial and appetising, without any useless complications. He must avoid, in his daily food, all that merely stuffs and causes heaviness; particularly he must be taught to eat according to his hunger, neither more nor less, and not to make food an occasion to satisfy his greed and gluttony. From one's very childhood, one should know that one eats in order to give to the body strength and health, and not to enjoy the pleasures of the palate. The child should be given the food that suits his temperament, prepared with all care for hygiene and cleanliness, pleasant to the taste and yet very simple; and this food should be chosen and measured out according to the age of the child and his regular activities; it must contain all the chemical and dynamic elements that are necessary for the development and the balanced growth of all the parts of the body.

Since the child will be given only the food needed for maintaining health and supplying necessary energy, one must be very careful not to use food as a means of coercion or punishment. The habit of telling a child: "You were not a good boy, you will not be given your dessert, etc." is totally disastrous. You create in this way in his little consciousness the impression that food is given to him chiefly to satisfy his greed and not because it is indispensable for the good functioning of his body.

Another thing should be taught to a child from his early

years: the taste for cleanliness and hygienic habits. But if you wish to form in the child this taste for cleanliness and respect for the rules of hygiene, you must take great care not to instil into him the fear of illness. Fear is the worst incentive for education and the surest way of attracting what is feared. Yet, while not fearing illness, one need have no inclination for it either. There is a current belief that brilliant minds have weak bodies. It is a delusion and has no basis. There was perhaps an epoch when a romantic and morbid taste for physical unbalance prevailed; but, fortunately, that tendency has disappeared. Nowadays a well-built, solid, muscular, strong and perfectly balanced body is appreciated at its true value. In any case, children should be taught to have respect for health, admiration for a healthy man whose body knows how to repel attacks of illness. Often a child pretends illness to escape a troublesome necessity, a work that does not interest him or even simply to move the heart of his parents and get them to satisfy some caprice. Children must also be taught, as early as possible, that this procedure is not worth the game and that they are not more interesting by being ill; rather the contrary. The weak have a tendency to believe that their weaknesses make them particularly interesting and to use this weakness and even their illness, if necessary, as means of attracting towards them the attention and sympathy of persons who are around them and live with them. On no account should this pernicious tendency be encouraged. Children should be taught that to be ill is a sign of failing and inferiority, not of a virtue or a sacrifice.

That is why it would be good for the child, as soon as he is able to make use of his limbs, to devote some time daily to developing methodically and normally all the parts of his body. Every day some twenty or thirty minutes, preferably on waking if possible, will suffice to assure the good functioning and balanced growth of his muscles, preventing at the same time stiffening of the joints and of the spine that comes about much earlier than it is supposed. In the general programme of education for children, sports and outdoor games should be given a fair place; that, more than all the medicines of the world, will assure them good health. An hour's moving about in the sun does more to cure weakness or anaemia than a whole armoury of tonics. My advice is that medicine should not be taken unless it is absolutely impossible to do otherwise; and this "absolutely impossible" must be absolutely strict. Although there are, in this programme of physical culture, certain well-known general lines as to how best to develop the human body, still if the method is to be fully effective, each case should be considered individually, if possible with the help of a competent person, otherwise by consulting books on the subject that have already been or are being published.

But in any case, a child, whatever may be his activities, should have a sufficient number of hours for sleep. This number will vary with age. In the cradle, the baby should sleep longer than it remains awake. The number of hours for sleep will diminish as the child grows. But till the adult age the number should not be less than eight hours and that in a quiet and well-ventilated place. The child should never be made to stay up uselessly. The hours before midnight are the best for resting the nerves. Even during the waking hours, relaxation is an indispensable thing for everyone who wishes to maintain the nervous balance. To know how to relax the muscles and the nerves is an art which should be taught to children even when very young. There are many parents who, on the contrary, force their children to constant activity. When the child remains quiet, they imagine he is ill. There are even parents who have the bad habit of making their child do household work at the expense of his rest and relaxation. Nothing is worse than that for a growing nervous system which cannot stand the tension of too continuous an effort or an activity imposed upon it and not freely chosen. I hold against all current ideas and prejudices that it is not fair to demand services from a child, as if it were his duty to serve his parents. The contrary would be more true: certainly it is natural that parents should serve their children, at least take great care of them. It is only if the child chooses freely to work for the family and does the work as a play that the thing is admissible. And even then, one must be careful that it diminishes in no way the hours of rest absolutely necessary for the body to function properly.

I said that even from a young age children should be taught respect for physical health, strength and balance. The great importance of beauty must also be insisted upon. A young child should aspire for beauty, not for the sake of pleasing others or gaining fame, but for the love of beauty itself: for beauty is the ideal which physical life has to realise. In every human being there is the possibility of establishing harmony among the different parts of the body and the different movements when the body is in action. The human body that undergoes a rational method of physical culture from the beginning of its existence can realise its own harmony and thus be fit to express beauty. When we shall speak of the other aspects of an integral education, we shall see what are the inner conditions to be fulfilled if this beauty is to be manifested one day.

Till now I have referred only to the education to be given to children; for, a good many bodily defects and malformations can be avoided by an enlightened physical education given at the proper time. But if, for some reason or other, this education has not been given during childhood and even in youth, it can begin at any age and followed throughout life. But the later one begins, the more one must be prepared to meet bad habits that have to be corrected, rigidities to be made supple, malformations to be rectified. And this preparatory work will need much patience and perseverance before one can start on a constructive programme for the harmonisation of the form and its movements. But if you hold within yourself the living ideal of beauty that is to be realised, you are sure to reach the goal you aim at.

IV

THE EDUCATION OF THE VITAL

Of all education, the education of the vital is perhaps the most important and the most indispensable. Yet it is rarely taken up and followed with understanding and method. There are several reasons for this: first, human thinking is in a great confusion over what concerns this particular subject; secondly, the enterprise is very difficult and to be successful in it one must have endurance, endless persistence and an inflexible will.

Indeed, the vital in man's nature is a despotic and exacting tyrant. Moreover, since it holds within itself power, energy, enthusiasm, effective dynamism, many have a feeling of timorous respect for it and try always to please it. But it is a master that is satisfied by nothing and its demands have no limit. Two ideas, very widespread, specially in the West, contribute towards making its domination ever more masterful. One is that the goal of life is to be happy; the other that you are born with a certain character and it is impossible to change it.

The first idea is a childish deformation of a very profound truth: it is that all existence is based upon the delight of being and without the delight of being there would be no life. But this delight of being, which is a quality of the Divine and therefore unconditioned, must not be confused with the pursuit of pleasure in life, for that depends largely upon circumstances. The conviction that makes one believe that one has the right to be happy leads, as a matter of course, towards the will to live one's life at any cost. This attitude in its obscure and aggressive egoism brings about every conflict and misery, deception and discouragement, ending often in a catastrophe.

In the world, as it actually is, the goal of life is not to secure personal happiness, but to awaken the individual progressively towards the Truth-consciousness.

The second idea arises from the fact that a fundamental change in character needs an almost complete mastery over the subconscient and a very rigorous disciplining of whatever comes up from the inconscient, which, in ordinary natures, is an expression of the consequences of atavism and of the environment in which one is born. Only an almost abnormal growth of consciousness and the constant help of Grace can achieve this Herculean task. Besides, this task has rarely been attempted; many famous teachers have declared it unrealisable and chimerical. Yet it is not unrealisable. The transformation of character has been realised in fact by means of a clear-sighted discipline and a perseverance so obstinate that nothing, not even the most persistent failures, can discourage it.

The indispensable starting-point is a detailed and discerning observation of the character to be transformed. In most cases, that itself is a difficult and often baffling task. But there is one fact which the old traditions knew and which can serve as the clew in the labyrinth of inner discovery. It is that everyone possesses in a large measure, and the exceptional individual in an increasing degree of precision, two opposite tendencies in the character, almost in equal proportions, which are like the light and the shadow of the same thing. Thus a man who has the capacity of being exceptionally generous suddenly finds rushing up in his nature an obstinate avarice; the courageous is somewhere a coward and the good suddenly have wicked impulses. Life seems to endow everyone, along with the possibility of expressing an ideal, with contrary elements representing in a concrete manner the battle he has to wage and the victory he has to win so that the realisation may be possible. In this way, all life is an education carried on more or less consciously, more or less deliberately. In certain cases this education helps the movements expressing the light, in others the opposite movements *i.e.*, those that express the shadow. If the circumstances and the environment are favourable, the light will grow at the expense of the shadow; otherwise the contrary will happen. Hence the individual's character will crystallise according to the caprice of nature and the determinism of a material and vital life, unless there is a luminous intervention of a higher element, a conscious will which will not let nature follow its whimsical procedure but replace it by a logical and clear-seeing discipline. This conscious will is what we mean by the rational method of education.

That is why it is of prime importance that the education of the child's vital should begin as early as possible, indeed, as soon as he is able to use his senses. In that way, many bad habits will be avoided and harmful influences eliminated.

The education of the vital has two principal aspects, very different as to the goal and the process, but both are equally important. The first is to develop and utilise the sense organs, the second is to become conscious and gradually master of one's character and in the end to achieve its transformation.

The education of the senses, again, has several aspects, adding to each other as the being grows: indeed this education should not stop at all. The sense organs may be so cultivated as to attain a precision and power in their functioning far greater than what is normally expected of them.

Some ancient mystic knowledge declared that the number of senses that man can develop is not five but seven and in certain special cases even twelve. Certain races at certain epochs have, through necessity, developed more or less perfectly one or the other of these supplementary senses. With a proper discipline persistently gone through, they are within the reach of all who are sincerely interested in their culture and its results. Among the many faculties that are often spoken of, there is, for example, this one: to widen the physical consciousness, project it out of oneself so as to concentrate on a definite point and thus get the sight, hearing, smell, taste and even the touch at a distance.

To this general education of the senses and their action there will be added, as early as possible, the cultivation of discrimination and the aesthetic sense, the capacity to choose and take up what is beautiful and harmonious, simple, healthy and pure. For, there is a psychological health even as there is a physical health; there is a beauty and harmony of the sensations, even as there is a beauty of the body and its movements. As the capacity of understanding grows in the child he should be taught, in the course of his education, to add artistic taste and refinement to power and precision. He must be shown, made to appreciate, taught to love beautiful, lofty, healthy and noble things, whether in nature or in human creation. It must be a true aesthetic culture and it will save him from degrading influences. For in the wake of the last wars and the terrible nervous tension which they provoked, as a sign, perhaps, of the decline of civilisation and decomposition of society, has come a growing vulgarity which seems to have taken possession of human life, individual as well as collective, particularly on the level of aesthetic life and the life of the senses. A methodical and enlightened cultivation of the senses can, little by little, remove from the child whatever is vulgar, commonplace and crude in him through contagion: this education will have happy reactions even on his character. For one who has developed a truly refined taste, will feel, because of this very refinement, incapable of acting in a crude, brutal or vulgar manner. This refinement, if it is sincere, will bring to the being a nobility and generosity which will spontaneously find expression in his behaviour and will keep him away from many base and perverse movements.

And this brings us naturally to the second aspect of vital education, *i.e.*, that which concerns character and its transformation.

Generally, systems of discipline dealing with the vital, its purification and its mastery proceed by coercion, suppression, abstinence and asceticism. The procedure is certainly easier and quicker although, in a deeper way, less enduring and effective than that of strict and detailed education. Besides, it eliminates all possibility of the intervention, help and collaboration of the vital. However, this help is of the utmost importance if one wishes to have an all-round growth of the individual and his activity.

To become conscious of the many movements in oneself and take note of what one does and why one does it, is the indispensable starting-point. The child must be taught to observe himself, to note his reactions and impulses and their causes, to become a clear-sighted witness of his desires, his movements of violence and passion, his instincts of possession and appropriation and domination and the background of vanity against which they stand with their counterparts of weakness, discouragement, depression and despair.

Evidently, the process would be useful only when along with the growth of the power of observation there grows also the will towards progress and perfection. This will is to be instilled into the child as soon as he is capable of having one, that is to say, at a much younger age than is usually believed.

There are different methods according to different cases for awakening this will to surmount and conquer: on certain individuals it is rational arguments that are effective, for others sentiment and goodwill are to be brought into play, in others again it is the sense of dignity and self-respect; for all, however, it is the example shown constantly and sincerely that is the most powerful means.

Once the resolution is firmly established, there is nothing more to do than to proceed with strictness and persistence, never to accept defeat as final. If you are to avoid all weakening and withdrawing, there is one important point you must know and never forget: the will can be cultivated and developed even like the muscles by methodical and progressive exercise. You must not shrink from demanding of your will the maximum effort even for a thing that appears to be of no importance; for it is by effort that capacity grows, acquiring little by little the power to apply itself even to the most difficult things. What you have decided to do, you must do, come what may, even if you have to begin your attempt over and over again any number of times. Your will will be strengthened by the effort, and in the end you will have nothing more to do than to choose with a clear vision the goal to which you will apply it.

To sum up: one must gain a full knowledge of one's character and then acquire control over one's movements so that one may achieve perfect mastery and transformation of all the elements that have to be transformed.

Now, all will depend upon the ideal which the effort for mastery and transformation seeks to achieve. The value of the effort and its result will depend upon the value of the ideal. This is the subject we shall deal with next, in connection with mental education.

V

MENTAL EDUCATION

Of all education, that of the mind is the best known and the most in use; yet except in a few rare cases, there are lacunae which make of it something very incomplete and, in the end, quite insufficient.

Generally speaking, education is taken to mean the required mental education. And when a child has been made to undergo, for a number of years, a course of severe training, which is more like stuffing the brain than educating it, it is considered that whatever is necessary for his mental growth has been done. But in reality nothing of the kind has been done. Even when the training is given with due measure and discrimination and does not impair the brain, it cannot impart to the human mind the faculties it needs to make a good and useful instrument. The education that is usually given can, at the most, serve as a gymnastic exercise to increase the suppleness of the brain. From this standpoint, each branch of human learning represents a special kind of mental gymnastics, and the verbal formulae used in each of these branches constitute, in each case, a special and well-defined language.

A true education of the mind, that which will prepare man for a higher life, has five principal phases. Normally these phases come one after another, but in exceptional individuals they may come alternately or even simultaneously. The five phases, in brief, are:

(1) Development of the power of concentration, the capacity of attention.

(2) Development of the capacities of expansion, wideness, complexity and richness.

(3) Organisation of ideas around a central idea or a higher ideal or a supremely luminous idea that will serve as a guide in life.

(4) Thought control, rejection of undesirable thoughts, so that one may, in the end, think only what one wants and when one wants it.

(5) Development of mental silence, perfect calm and a more and more total receptivity to inspirations coming from the higher regions of the being.

It is not possible to give here all the details concerning the methods to be employed in the application of these phases of education to different individuals. Still some explanatory indications can be given.

It cannot be gainsaid that what most impedes mental progress in the child is the constant dispersion of his thoughts. His thought flutters hither and thither like a butterfly and a great effort is required on his part to fix it. Yet the capacity is latent in him for when you succeed in making him interested, he is capable of a good deal of attention. It is therefore the skill of the educator that will gradually make the child capable of a sustained effort of attention and a faculty of more and more complete absorption in the work while it is being done. All means are good that can develop this faculty of attention: they can all be utilised according to need and circumstances, from games up to rewards. But it is the psychological action that is most important and the sovereign means is to rouse in the child interest in the thing that one wishes to teach, the taste for work, the will to progress. To love to learn is the most precious gift that one can make to a child: to love to learn always and everywhere. Let all circumstances, all happenings in life be occasions, constantly renewed, for learning more and ever more.

For that, to attention and concentration should be added observation, precision of recording and faithfulness of memory. This faculty of observation can be developed by various and spontaneous exercises, making use of all opportunities that help to keep the child's thought wakeful, alert, quick. The growth of the understanding much more than that of memory should be insisted upon. One knows only what one understands. Things learnt by heart, mechanically, get blurred little by little and finally fade away: you never forget what you understand. Moreover, you must never refuse to explain to a child the how and the why of things. If you cannot do it yourself, you must direct the child to those qualified to answer him or to books dealing with the question. It is in this way that you will progressively awake in the child the taste for real study and the habit of a persistent effort to know.

This will take us naturally to the second phase of growth in which the mind has to be enlarged and enriched.

As the child progresses you will show him how everything can become an interesting subject for study, provided the question is approached in the right manner. The life of every day, of every moment is the best of all schools, varied, complex, rich in unforeseen experiences, in problems awaiting solution, in clear and striking examples and in evident consequences. It is so easy to rouse healthy curiosity in children, if you answer with intelligence and clarity the numberless questions they put. An interesting reply brings in its train others and the child, his attention attracted, learns without effort much more than what he usually does on the school bench. A careful and intelligent selection should also give him a taste for healthy reading which is at once instructive and attractive. Fear nothing that awakes and satisfies his imagination; it is imagination that develops the creative mental faculty and it is through that that study becomes a living thing and the mind grows in joy.

In order to increase the suppleness and comprehensiveness of his mind, one should not only look to the number and variety of subjects for study, but particularly to the diverse approaches to the same subject; by this means the child will be made to understand in a practical way that there are many ways of facing the same intellectual problem, dealing with it and solving it. The brain will thus be free from all rigidity and, at the same time, thought will gain in richness and suppleness and be made ready for a more complex and comprehensive synthesis. In this way also the child will be imbued with the sense of the extreme relativity of mental knowledge and, little by little, an aspiration will be awakened in him for a truer source of knowledge.

Indeed, as the child progresses in his studies and grows in age, his mind too ripens and is more and more capable of general ideas; and along with this, there always comes the need for certitude, for a knowledge stable enough to be made the basis of a mental construction which will permit all diverse and scattered and often contradictory ideas accumulated in the brain to be organised and put in order. This ordering is indeed very necessary if one is to avoid chaos in one's thoughts. All contradictories can be transformed into complementaries, but for that one must discover a higher idea that will be able to harmonise them. It is good to consider all problems from all possible standpoints to avoid partiality and exclusiveness, but if the thought is to be active and creative it must, in each case, be the natural and logical synthesis of all the points of view taken in. And if you are to make of the totality of your thoughts a dynamic and constructive force, you must take great care as to the choice of the central idea of your mental synthesis; for upon that will depend the value of your synthesis. The higher and larger the central idea and the more universal it is, rising above time and space, the more numerous and the more complex will be the ideas, notions and thoughts which it will be able to organise and harmonise.

It goes without saying that the work of organisation cannot be done all at once. The mind, if it is to keep its vigour and youth, must progress constantly, revise its notions in the light of all new knowledge, enlarge its frame to include fresh notions and constantly reclassify and reorganise its thoughts, so that each one of them may find its proper place in relation to others and the whole thus stand harmonious and orderly.

All that has just been said, however, concerns the speculative mind, the mind that learns. But learning is only one aspect of mental activity; the other, at least as important, is the constructive faculty, the capacity to give form and therefore prepare for action. This part of mental activity, although very important, has rarely been the subject of any special study and discipline. Only those who want, for some reason, to exercise a strict control over their mental activities think of observing and disciplining this faculty of formation; even so, as soon as they try it, they find themselves faced with such great difficulties that they appear almost insurmountable.

And yet control over this formative activity of the mind is one of the most important aspects of self-education: one can say that without it no mental mastery is possible. On the side of study, all ideas are acceptable and should be included in the synthesis whose very function is to become more and more rich and complex; but, on the side of action, it is quite the contrary. A strict control should be put on ideas that are accepted for translation into action and only those that agree with the general trend of the central idea forming the basis of the mental synthesis should be permitted to express themselves in action. This means that every thought entering the mental consciousness should be placed before the central idea; if it finds a right place among the thoughts already grouped, it will be admitted into the synthesis; if not, it will be thrown out, so that it cannot have any influence upon the action. This work of mental purification should be done very regularly to secure a complete control over one's actions.

For that purpose, it is good to set apart every day some time when one can quietly go over one's thoughts and put order into one's synthesis. Once the habit is acquired, you can maintain your control over thoughts even during work and action and you will be able not to let any come to the fore that is not useful to the thing undertaken. Particularly if the power of concentration and attention is continuously cultivated, the active external consciousness will allow only those thoughts that are needed and then they become all the more dynamic and effective. And if, in the intensity of concentration, it is necessary not to think at all, all mental vibration can be stopped and an almost total silence secured. In this silence one can open gradually to the higher mental regions and learn to record the inspirations that come from there.

But even before arriving at this point, silence in itself is

supremely useful because in most people who have a some-
what developed and active mind, the mind is never at rest.
During the day, its activity is put under a certain control,
but at night, during the sleep of the body, the control of
the waking state is almost completely removed and the
mind indulges in excessive and often incoherent activities.
This creates a great tension ending in fatigue and diminu-
tion of mental faculties.

The fact is that, like all the other parts of the human being,
the mind too needs rest and this rest it will not have unless
we know how to give it. The art of giving rest to one's mind
is a thing to be acquired. Changing mental activity is a way
of rest; but the greatest possible rest lies in silence. And
in the case of mental faculties, a few minutes passed in the
calm of silence mean a more effective rest than hours of
sleep.

When one will have learnt to silence the mind at will
and concentrate it in the receptive silence, then there will
be no problem that one cannot solve, no mental difficulty
to which a solution will not be found. Thought, while in
agitation, becomes confused and impotent; in an attentive
tranquillity, the light can manifest itself and open new
horizons to man's capacity.

VI

PSYCHIC AND SPIRITUAL EDUCATION

Till now we have dealt with the education which can be given to all children born upon earth; it is concerned with purely human faculties. But one need not stop there. Every human being carries hidden within him the possibility of a greater consciousness beyond the frame of his normal life through which he can participate in a higher and vaster life. Indeed, in all exceptional beings it is always this consciousness that governs their life, and organises both the circumstances of their life and their individual reaction to these circumstances. What the human mind does not know and cannot do, this consciousness knows and does. It is like a light that shines at the centre of the being radiating through the thick coverings of the external consciousness. Some have a vague perception of its presence; a good many children are under its influence which shows itself very distinctly at times in their spontaneous actions and even in their words. Unfortunately parents most often do not know what it is and do not understand what is happening in their children; therefore their reaction with regard to these phenomena is not happy and all their education consists in making the child as unconscious as possible in this domain to concentrate all its attention upon external things, thus forming the habit of looking upon those alone as important. It is true that this concentration upon external things is very useful; provided it is done in the proper way. The three lines of education — physical, vital and mental — deal with that which may be defined as the means of building up the personality, raising the individual out of the amorphous subconscious mass, making it a well-defined self-conscious entity. With psychic education we come to the problem of the true motive of life, the reason of our existence upon earth, the discovery to which life must lead and the result of that discovery: the consecration of the individual to his eternal principle. This discovery very generally is associated with a mystic feeling, a religious life, because it is religions particularly that have been occupied with this aspect of life. But it need not be necessarily so: the mystic notion of God may be replaced by the more philosophical notion of truth and still the discovery will remain essentially the same, only the road leading to it may be taken even by the most intransigent positivist. For mental notions and ideas possess a very secondary importance in preparing one for the psychic life. The important thing is to live the experience: for it carries its own reality and force apart from any theory that may precede or accompany or follow it, because most often theories are mere explanations that are given to oneself in order to have more or less the illusion of knowledge. Man clothes the ideal or the absolute he seeks to attain with different names according to the environment in which he is born and the education he has received. The experience is essentially the same, if it is sincere; it is only the words and phrases in which it is formulated that differ according to the belief and the mental education of the one who has the experience. All formulation is only an approximation that should be progressive and grow in precision as the experience itself becomes more and more precise and co-ordinated. Still, if we are to give a general outline of psychic education, we must have an idea, however relative it may be, of what we mean by the psychic being. Thus one can say, for example, that the creation of an individual being is the result of the projection, in time and space, of one of the countless possibilities latent in the Supreme Origin of all manifestation which, through the one and universal consciousness, is concretised in the law or the truth of an individual and so becomes by a progressive growth its soul or psychic being.

I stress the point that what I have said here in brief does not profess to be a complete exposition of the reality and does not exhaust the subject — far from it. It is just a summary explanation for a practical purpose so that it can serve as a basis for the education with which we are concerned.

It is through the psychic presence that the truth of an individual being comes into contact with him and the circumstances of his life. In most cases this presence acts, so to say, from behind the veil, unrecognised and unknown; but in some, it is perceptible and its action recognisable; even, in a few among these, the presence becomes tangible and its action quite effective. These go forward in their life with an assurance and a certitude all their own, they are masters of their destiny. It is precisely with a view to obtain this mastery and become conscious of the psychic presence that psychic education has to be pursued. But for that there is need of a special factor, the personal will. For till now, the discovery of the psychic being, the identification with it, has not been among the recognised subjects of education. It is true one can find in special treatises useful and practical hints on the subject, and also there are persons fortunate enough to meet someone capable of showing the path and giving the necessary help to follow it. More often, however, the attempt is left to one's own personal initiative: the discovery is a personal matter and a great resolution, a strong will and an untiring perseverance are indispensable to reach the goal. Each one must, so to say, chalk out his own path through his own difficulties. The goal is known to some extent; for, most of those who have reached it have described it more or less clearly. But the supreme value of the discovery lies in its spontaneity, its genuineness: that escapes all ordinary mental laws. And this is why anyone wanting to take up the adventure, usually seeks at first some person who has gone through it successfully and is able to sustain him and show him the way. Yet there are some solitary travellers and for them a few general indications may be useful.

The starting-point is to seek in yourself that which is independent of the body and the circumstances of life, which is not born of the mental formation that you have been given, the language you speak, the habits and customs of the environment in which you live, the country where you are born or the age to which you belong. You must find, in the depths of your being, that which carries in it the sense of universality, limitless expansion, termless continuity. Then you decentralise, spread out, enlarge yourself; you begin to live in everything and in all beings; the barriers separating individuals from each other break down. You think in their thoughts, vibrate in their sensations, you feel in their feelings, you live in the life of all. What seemed inert suddenly becomes full of life, stones quicken, plants feel and will and suffer, animals speak in a language more or less inarticulate, but clear and expressive; everything is animated with a marvellous consciousness without time and limit. And this is only one aspect of the psychic realisation. There are many others. All combine in pulling you out of the barriers of your egoism, the walls of your external personality, the impotence of your reactions and the incapacity of your will.

But, as I have already said, the path to come to that realisation is long and difficult, strewn with traps and problems, and to face them demands a determination that must be equal to all test and trial. It is like the explorer's journey through virgin forest, in quest of an unknown land, towards great discovery. The psychic being is also a great discovery to be made requiring at least as much fortitude and endurance as the discovery of new continents. A few words of advice may be useful to one resolved to undertake it:

The first and perhaps the most important point is that the mind is incapable of judging spiritual things. All those who have written on Yogic discipline have said so; but very few are those who have put it into practice and yet, in order to proceed on the path, it is absolutely indispensable to abstain from all mental opinion and reaction.

Give up all personal seeking for comfort, satisfaction, enjoyment or happiness. Be only a burning fire for progress, take whatever comes to you as a help for progress and make at once the progress required.

Try to take pleasure in all you do, but never do anything for the sake of pleasure.

Never get excited, nervous or agitated. Remain perfectly quiet in the face of all circumstances. And yet be always awake to find out the progress you have still to make and lose no time in making it.

Never take physical happenings at their face value. They are always a clumsy attempt to express something else, the true thing which escapes your superficial understanding.

Never complain of the behaviour of anyone, unless you have the power to change in his nature what makes him act thus; and if you have the power, change him instead of complaining.

Whatever you do, never forget the goal which you have set before you. There is nothing small or big in this enterprise of a great discovery; all things are equally important and can either hasten or delay its success. Thus before you eat, concentrate a few seconds in the aspiration that the food you will take brings to your body the substance necessary to serve as a solid basis for your effort towards the great discovery, and gives it the energy of persistence and perseverance in the effort.

Before you go to bed, concentrate a few seconds in the aspiration that the sleep may restore your fatigued nerves, bring to your brain calmness and quietness, that on waking up you may, with renewed vigour, begin again your journey on the path of the great discovery.

Before you act, concentrate in the will that your action may help, at least not hinder in any way, your march forward towards the great discovery.

When you speak, before the words come out of your mouth, concentrate awhile just long enough to check your words and allow those alone that are absolutely necessary and are not in any way harmful to your progress on the path of the great discovery.

In brief, never forget the purpose and the goal of your life. The will for the great discovery should be always there soaring over you, above what you do and what you are, like a huge bird of light dominating all the movements of your being.

Before the untiring persistence of your effort, an inner door will open suddenly and you will come out into a dazzling splendour that will bring to you the certitude of immortality, the concrete experience that you have lived always and always shall live, that the external forms alone perish and that these forms are, in relation to what you are in reality, like clothes that are thrown away when worn out. Then you will stand erect freed from all chains and instead of advancing with difficulty under the load of circumstances imposed upon you by nature, borne and suffered by you, if you do not want to be crushed under them, you can walk on straight and firm, conscious of your destiny, master of your life.

And yet this release from all slavery to the flesh, this liberation from all personal attachment is not the supreme fulfilment. There are other steps to climb before you reach the summit. And even these steps can and should be followed by others which will open the gates of the future. It is these later steps that will be the subject-matter of what I call spiritual education.

But before we enter this new stage and deal with the question in detail, an explanation is necessary. Why is there a distinction made between the psychic education of which we have just spoken and the spiritual education of which we are going to speak presently? Because the two are usually mixed up under the generic name "yogic discipline", although the goal they aim at is very different in each case: for one, it is a higher realisation upon earth, for the other, an escape from all earthly manifestation, even away from the whole universe, a return to the unmanifest.

So one can say that the psychic life is the life immortal, endless time, limitless space, ever-progressive change, unbroken continuity in the world of forms. The spiritual consciousness, on the other hand, means to live the infinite and eternal, to throw oneself outside all creation, beyond time and space. To become fully aware of your psychic being and to live a psychic life you must abolish in you all selfishness; but to live a spiritual life you must be selfless.

Here also in spiritual education, the goal you set before you will assume, in the mind's formulation of it, different names according to the environment in which you have grown, the path you have followed and the affinities of your temperament. If you have a religious tendency you will call it God and your spiritual effort will be towards identification with the transcendent God beyond all forms, in opposition to the Immanent God dwelling in each form. Others will call it the Absolute, the Supreme Origin, others again, Nirvana; yet others who view the world as an unreal illusion will name it the Only Reality and to those who regard all manifestation as falsehood it will be the Sole Truth. And every one of these definitions contains an element of truth, but all are incomplete, expressing only one aspect of what is. Here also the mental formulation has no great importance and once you cross the intermediate stages, it is always the same experience. In any case, the most effective starting-point, the swiftest method is total self-surrender. Besides, no joy is more perfect than that of a total self-surrender to the highest point your conception can reach: for some it is the notion of God, for others that of Perfection. If this surrender is made with persistence and ardour, a moment comes when you go beyond the concept and arrive at an experience that escapes all description, but which is almost always identical in its effects. As your surrender becomes more and more perfect and integral, it will carry with it the aspiration for identification, a total fusion with That to which you have given yourself, and little by little this aspiration will overcome all differences and all resistances, especially if the aspiration has, added to it, an intense and spontaneous love for then nothing can stand in the way of its victorious onset.

There is an essential difference between this identification and the one with the psychic being. The latter can be made more and more durable and, in certain cases, it becomes permanent and never leaves the person who has realised it, whatever may be his outer activities. In other words, the identification is no more realised only in meditation and concentration, but its effect can be felt at every moment of one's life, in sleep as well as in waking.

On the contrary, liberation from all form and identification with that which is beyond form cannot last in an absolute manner; for it would automatically bring about the dissolution of the material form. Certain traditions say that this dissolution happens inevitably within twenty days of the total identification. Yet it is not necessarily so; and even if the experience is only momentary, it produces in the consciousness results that are never obliterated and have repercussions on all the levels of the being, both internal and external. Moreover, once the identification has been realised, it can be renewed at will, provided you know how to put yourself in the same conditions.

This merging into the formless is the supreme liberation sought by those who want to escape from existence which has no attraction for them any more. It is nothing surprising that they are not satisfied with the world in its present form. But a liberation that leaves the world as it is and does in no way affect the conditions of life from which others suffer, cannot satisfy those who refuse to live in a felicity which they alone enjoy, and who dream of a world more worthy of the splendours that hide behind its apparent disorder and general misery. They dream of making others profit by the wonders they have discovered in their inner exploration. And the means to do so is within their reach, now that they have arrived at the summit of their ascent.

From beyond the frontiers of form, a new force can be evoked, a power of consciousness which has not yet manifested and which, by its emergence, will be able to change the course of things and bring to birth a new world. For the true solution of the problem of suffering, ignorance and death is not the individual escape by self-annihilation from earthly miseries into the non-manifest, nor a problematical collective flight from universal suffering by an integral and final return of the creation to its creator, thus curing the universe by abolishing it, but a transformation, a total transfiguration of matter brought about by the logical continuation of Nature's ascending march in her progress towards perfection, by the creation of a new species that will be in relation to man what man is in relation to the animal and that will manifest upon earth a new force, a new consciousness and a new power. Then will begin also a new education which can be called the supramental education; it will, by its all-powerful action, work not only upon the consciousness of individual beings, but upon the very substance of which they are built and upon the environment in which they live.

Contrary to the type of education we have spoken of hitherto that progresses from below upward through an ascending movement of the different parts of the being, the supramental education will progress from above downward, its influence spreading from one state of being to another till the final state, the physical, is reached. This last transformation will happen in a visible manner only when the inner states of being have already been considerably transformed. It is therefore quite unreasonable to try to judge the presence of the supramental through physical appearances. The physical is the last to change and the supramental force can be at work in a being long before something of it becomes perceptible in the life of the body.

In brief, one can say that the supramental education will result not merely in a progressively developing formation of the human nature, an increasing growth of its latent faculties, but a transformation of the nature itself, a transfiguration of the being in its entirety, a new ascent of the species above and beyond man towards superman, leading in the end to the appearance of a divine race upon earth.

FOUR AUSTERITIES AND FOUR LIBERATIONS*

I

To pursue an integral education that leads to the supramental realisation a fourfold austerity is necessary and also a fourfold liberation.

Austerity is usually confused with mortification. When austerity is spoken of, one thinks of the discipline of the ascetic who seeks to avoid the arduous task of spiritualising the physical, vital and mental life and therefore declares it incapable of transformation and casts it away without pity as a useless burden, a bondage fettering all spiritual progress; in any case, it is considered as a thing that cannot be mended, a load that has to be borne more or less cheerfully until the time when Nature or the Divine Grace relieves you of it by death. At best life on earth is a field for progress and one should try to get the utmost profit out of it, all the sooner to reach that degree of perfection which will put an end to the trial by making it unnecessary.

For us the problem is quite different. Life on earth is not a passage nor a means merely; it must become, through transformation, a goal, a realisation. When we speak of austerity, it is not out of contempt for the body, with a view to dissociating ourselves from it, but because of the need of self-control and self-mastery. For, there is an austerity which is far greater, more complete and more difficult than all the austerities of the ascetic: the austerity necessary for the integral transformation, the fourfold austerity

* Reprinted from the *Bulletin of Physical Education*, Feb. to Aug. 1953 (Sri Aurobindo Ashram, Pondicherry).

which prepares the individual for the manifestation of the supramental truth. One can say, for example, that few austerities are so severe as those which physical culture demands for the perfection of the body. But of that we shall speak in due time.

Before I begin describing the four kinds of austerity required, I must clear up one question which is a source of much misunderstanding and confusion in the minds of most people: it is about ascetic practices which they mistake for spiritual discipline. Now, these practices consist in ill-treating the body so that one may, as it is said, free the spirit from it; they are, in fact, a sensual deformation of spiritual discipline; it is a kind of perverse need for suffering that drives the ascetic to self-mortification. The Sadhu's "bed of nails" and the Christian anchorite's whip and sack-cloth are the results of a sadism, more or less veiled, unavowed and unavowable; it is an unhealthy seeking or a subconscient need for violent sensations. In reality, these things are very far from the spiritual life; for they are ugly and low, dark and diseased; spiritual life, on the contrary, is a life of light and balance, beauty and joy. They have been invented and extolled by a sort of mental and vital cruelty inflicted on the body. But cruelty, even with regard to one's own body, is none the less cruelty, and all cruelty is a sign of great unconsciousness. Unconscious natures need very strong sensations; for without that they feel nothing; and cruelty, being a form of sadism, brings very strong sensations. The avowed purpose of such practices is to abolish all sensation so that the body may no longer be an obstacle to one's flight towards the Spirit; the efficacy of such means is open to doubt. It is a well-known fact that if one wants quick progress one must not be afraid of difficulties; on the contrary, it is by choosing to do the difficult thing each time the occasion presents itself that one increases the will and strengthens the nerves. Indeed, it is much more difficult to lead a life of measure and balance, equanimity and serenity than to fight the abuses of pleasure and the obscuration they cause, by the abuses of asceticism and the disintegration they bring about. It is much more difficult to secure a harmonious and progressive growth in calmness and simplicity in one's physical being than to ill-treat it to the point of reducing it to nothing. It is much more difficult to live soberly and without desire than to deprive the body of nourishment and clean habits so indispensable to it, just to show off proudly one's abstinence. It is much more difficult again to avoid, surmount or conquer illness by an inner and outer harmony, purity and balance than to despise and ignore it, leaving it free do its work of ruin. And the most difficult thing of all is to maintain the consciousness always on the peak of its capacity and never allow the body to act under the influence of a lower impulse.

It is with this end in view that we should adopt the four austerities which will result in the four liberations. Their practice will constitute the fourfold discipline or Tapasya which can be thus defined:

(1) Tapasya of Love.
(2) Tapasya of Knowledge.
(3) Tapasya of Power.
(4) Tapasya of Beauty.

The gradation is, so to say, from above downwards; but the steps, as they stand, should not be taken to mean anything superior or inferior, nor more or less difficult nor the order in which these disciplines can be and should be followed. The order, importance, difficulty vary according to the individual and no absolute rule can be framed. Each one should find and work out his own system, according to his capacity and personal needs.

Only an overall view will be given here presenting an ideal procedure that is as complete as possible. Everyone will then have to apply it as far as he can and as best he can.

The Tapasya or discipline of beauty will take us through the austerity of physical life, to freedom in action. The basic programme will be to build a body, beautiful in form, harmonious in posture, supple and agile in its movements, powerful in its activities and resistant in its health and organic function.

To get these results it will be good, in a general way, to form habits and utilise them as a help in organising the material life. For the body works more easily in a frame of regular routine. Yet one must know how not to become a slave to one's habits, however good they may be. The greatest suppleness must be maintained so that one may change one's habits each time it is necessary to do so.

One must build up nerves of steel in a system of elastic and strong muscles, so that one is capable of enduring anything whenever it is indispensable. But at the same time care must be taken not to ask of the body more than the strictly necessary amount of effort, the energy required for growth and progress, and shut out most strictly all that produces exhausting fatigue and leads in the end to degeneration and decomposition of the material elements.

Physical culture which aims at building a body capable of serving as a fit instrument for the higher consciousness demands very austere habits: a great regularity in sleep, food, physical exercises and in all activities. One should study scrupulously the needs of one's body — for these vary according to individuals — and then fix a general programme. Once the programme is fixed, one must stick to it rigorously with no fancifulness or slackness : none of those exceptions to the rule indulged in "just for once", but which are repeated often — for, when you yield to temptation even "just for once", you lessen the resistance of your will and open the door to each and every defeat. You must put a bar to all weakness; none of the nightly escapades from which you come back totally broken, no feasting and glutting which disturb the normal working of the stomach, no distraction, dissipation or merry-making that only waste energy and leave you too lifeless to do the daily practice. One must go through the austerity of a wise and well-regulated life, concentrating the whole physical attention upon building a body as perfect as it is possible for it to become. To reach this ideal goal one must strictly shun all excess, all vice, small or big, one must deny oneself the use of such slow poisons as tobacco, alcohol, etc. which men have the habit of developing into indispensable needs that gradually demolish their will and memory. The all-absorbing interest that men, without exception, even the most intellectual, take in food, in its preparation and consumption, should be replaced by an almost chemical knowledge of the needs of the body and a wholly scientific system of austerity in the way of satisfying them. One must add to this austerity regarding food, another austerity, that of sleep. It does not mean that one should go without sleep, but that one must know how to sleep. Sleep must not be a fall into unconsciousness that makes the body heavy instead of refreshing it. Moderate food, abstention from all excess, by itself minimises considerably the necessity of passing many hours in sleep. However, it is the quality of sleep more than its quantity that is important. If sleep is to bring you truly effective rest and repose, it would be good to take something before going to bed, a cup of milk or soup or fruit-juice, for instance. Light food gives a quiet sleep. In any case, one must abstain from too much food; for that makes sleep troubled and agitated with nightmares or otherwise makes it dense, heavy and dull. But the most important thing is to keep the mind clear, to quiet the feelings, calm the effervescence of desires and preoccupations accompanying them. If before retiring to bed one has talked much, held animated discussions or read something intensely interesting and exciting, then one had better take some time to rest before sleeping so that the mind's activities may be quieted and the brain not yield to disorderly movements while the physical limbs alone sleep. If you are given to meditation, you would do well to concentrate for a few minutes upon a high and restful idea, in an aspiration towards a greater and vaster consciousness. Your sleep will profit greatly by it and you will escape in a large measure the risk of falling into unconsciousness while asleep.

After the austerity of a night passed wholly in rest, in a calm and peaceful sleep, comes the austerity of a day organised with wisdom, its activities divided between wisely graded progressive exercises, required for the culture of the body and the kind of work you do. For both can and should form part of the physical Tapasya. With regard to exercises, each one should choose what suits best his body and, if possible, under the guidance of an expert on the subject who knows how to combine and grade the exercises for their maximum effect. No fancifulness should rule their choice or execution. You should not do this or that simply because it appears more easy or pleasant; you will make a change in your programme only when your trainer considers the change necessary. The body of each one, with regard to its perfection or simply improvement, is a problem to be solved and the solution demands much patience, perseverance and regularity. In spite of what men may think, the athlete's life is not a life of pleasure and distraction; it is a life, on the contrary, made up of well-regulated endeavour and austere habits for getting the desired result and leaves no room for useless and harmful fancies.

In work too there is an austerity; it consists in not having any preference and in doing with interest whatever one does. For the man who wishes to perfect himself, there is nothing like small or big work, important work or unimportant. All are equally useful to him who aspires for self-mastery and progress. It is said that you do well only what you do with interest. True, but what is more true is that one can learn to find interest in whatever one does, even the work that appears most insignificant. The secret of this attainment lies in the urge towards perfection. Whatever be the occupation or task that falls to your lot, do it with a will towards progress. Whatever you do must be done not only as well as you can but with an earnestness to do it better and better in a constant drive towards perfection. In this way all things without exception become interesting, from the most material labour to the most artistic and intellectual work. The scope for progress is infinite and one can be earnest in the smallest thing.

This takes us naturally to liberation in action; for in one's action one must be free from all social conventions, all moral prejudices. This is not to say that one should lead a life of licence and unrule. On the contrary, you submit here to a rule which is much more severe than all social rules, for it does not tolerate any hypocrisy, it demands perfect sincerity. All physical activities should be organised in such a way as to make the body grow in balance and strength and beauty. With this end in view one must abstain from all pleasure-seeking, including the sexual pleasure. For each sexual act is a step towards death. That is why from the very ancient times among all the most sacred and most secret schools, this was a prohibited act for every aspirant to immortality. It is always followed by a more or less long spell of inconscience that opens the door to all kinds of influences and brings about a fall in the consciousness. Indeed, one who wants to prepare for the supramental life should never allow his consciousness to slip down to dissipation and inconscience under the pretext of enjoyment or even rest and relaxation. The relaxation should be into force and light, not into obscurity and weakness. Continence therefore is the rule for all who aspire for progress. But especially for those who want to prepare themselves for the supramental manifestation, this continence must be replaced by total abstinence, gained not by coercion and suppression but by a kind of inner alchemy through which the energies usually used in the act of procreation are transmuted into energies for progress and integral transformation. It goes without saying that to get a full and truly beneficial result, all sex impulse and desire must be eliminated from the mental and vital consciousness as well as from the physical will. All transformation that is radical and durable proceeds from within outwards, the outward transformation being the normal and, so to say, the inevitable result of the inner.

A decisive choice has to be made between lending the body to Nature's ends in obedience to her demand to perpetuate the race as it is, and preparing this very body to become a step towards the creation of the new race. For the two cannot go together; at every minute you have to decide whether you wish to remain within the humanity of yesterday or belong to the supermanhood of tomorrow. You must refuse to be moulded according to life as it is and be successful in it, if you want to prepare for life as it will be and become an active and efficient member of it. You must deny yourself pleasures, if you wish to be open to the joy of living in integral beauty and harmony.

This brings us quite naturally to vital austerity, the austerity of the sensations, the Tapasya of power; for the vital being is indeed the seat of power, of enthusiasms that realise. It is in the vital that thought changes into will and becomes a dynamism of action. It is also true that the vital is the seat of desires and passions, of violent impulses and equally violent reactions, of revolt and depression. The usual remedy is to strangle it, to starve it by depriving it of sensations: indeed it is nourished chiefly by sensations and without them it goes to sleep, becomes dull and insensitive and, in the end, wholly empty.

The vital, in fact, draws its subsistence from three sources.

The one most easily accessible to it is from below, the physical energies coming through the sensations. The second is on its own plane, when it is sufficiently wide and receptive, in contact with the universal vital forces. And the third, to which generally it opens only under a great aspiration for progress, comes from above through the infusion and absorption of spiritual forces and inspirations.

To these men try more or less always to add another

source; which is, at the same time, for them the source of most of their torments and misfortunes. It is the interchange of vital forces with their fellow creatures, generally grouped by twos, which they mistake for love, but which is only an attraction between two forces that take pleasure in mutual interchange.

So, if we do not wish to starve our vital, the sensations should not be rejected, nor reduced in number or blunted in intensity; neither should they be avoided, but they must be utilised with discrimination and discernment. Sensations are an excellent instrument for knowledge and education. To make them serve this purpose, they should not be used egoistically for the sake of enjoyment, in a blind and ignorant seeking for pleasure and self-satisfaction.

The senses should be able to bear everything without disgust or displeasure; at the same time they must acquire and develop more and more the power to discriminate the quality, origin and result of various vital vibrations, so as to know whether they are favourable to the harmony, the beauty and the good health or are harmful to the poise and progress of the physical and vital being. Moreover, the senses should be utilised as instruments to approach and study the physical and vital worlds in all their complexity. Thus they will take their true place in the great endeavour towards transformation.

It is by enlightening, strengthening and purifying the vital and not by weakening it that one can help towards the true progress of the being. To deprive oneself of sensations is therefore as harmful as depriving oneself of food. But even as the choice of food must be made with wisdom and only with a view to the growth and proper functioning of the body, so the choice of sensations also should be made and control over them gained with an altogether scientific austerity, with a view only to the growth and perfection of this great dynamic instrument which is as essential for progress as all the other parts of the being.

It is by educating the vital, by making it more refined, more sensitive, more subtle, one should almost say, more elegant, in the best sense of the word, that one can overcome its violences and brutalities which are, in general, movements of crudity and ignorance, of a lack of taste.

In reality, the vital, when educated and illumined, can be as noble, heroic and unselfish, as it is now spontaneously, vulgar, egoistic, perverted when left to itself without education. It is sufficient for each one to know how to transform in oneself this seeking for pleasure into an aspiration towards supramental plenitude. For that, if the education of the vital is pursued far enough, with perseverance and sincerity, there comes a moment when it is convinced of the greatness and beauty of the goal and gives up petty illusory satisfactions of the senses in order to conquer the divine Delight.

II

When we speak of mental austerity, the thing immediately suggested is long meditations leading to control of thought and finally to inner silence as the crown. This aspect of Yogic discipline is too well known to need dwelling upon at length. But there is another aspect with which people are generally less concerned: it is the control of speech. Apart from a very few exceptions, it is absolute silence that is put against unbridled talkativeness. Yet it is a much greater and more fruitful austerity to control one's speech than to abolish it altogether.

Man is the first animal upon earth to be able to use the articulate sound. He is indeed proud of it and exercises this capacity without measure or discrimination. The world is deafened with the noise of his speech and at times you almost seem to miss the harmonious silence of the vegetable kingdom.

It is besides a well-known fact that the less the mental power the greater is the need for speech. There are, for example, primitive people, people with no education, who cannot think at all without speaking; you can hear them muttering sounds in a more or less low voice. For it is the only means they have to follow the train of their thought which would not be formulated in them without articulated words.

There are also a large number of people and even among the educated those with weak mental power who do not know what they have to say except in the course of saying it. That makes their talk interminable and tedious. But while they speak, their thoughts get more and more clear and precise: and this impels them to repeat the same thing over and over again in order to be able to say it more and more exactly.

There are some who need preparing beforehand what they have to say; they falter if they are to speak on the spur of the moment, since they have not had the time to work out step by step the exact terms of what they wanted to say.

Lastly, there are the born orators who are masters of elocution; they spontaneously find the words needed to say what they mean and they say it well.

All that, however, from the point of view of mental austerity, does not fall outside the category of talkativeness. For by talkativeness I mean uttering any word that is not absolutely indispensable. How to judge? one may ask. For that, we have to classify in a general way all the categories of the spoken word.

First, we have in the physical domain all words uttered for a material reason. They are by far the most numerous and in ordinary life very probably the most useful.

The constant buzz of words seems to be the indispensable accompaniment of the daily routine work. Yet if you just endeavour to reduce the noise to a minimum, you begin to see that many things are done better and quicker in silence and this helps also to maintain the inner peace and concentration.

If you are not alone and you live with others, cultivate the habit not to throw yourself out constantly into spoken words. You will see that little by little an inner understanding is established between you and the others; you will then be able to communicate with each other with the minimum speech or no speech at all. This outer silence is very favourable to inner peace and if you have good will

and constant aspiration you will be able to create a harmonious atmosphere conducive to progress.

In a community life, to words concerning the daily life
and material preoccupations are to be added also those
that express sensations, feelings and emotions. It is here
that the habit of external silence comes as a precious help.
For when you are assailed by a wave of sensations or feelings, it is this habit of silence that gives you time to reflect
and, if necessary, control yourself before you throw out
into words your sensations and your feelings. How many
quarrels can be avoided in this way! How many times would
you be saved from one of those psychological catastrophes
which are but too often the result of incontinence in speech.

Even if you do not go to this extreme, you should always
control the words you utter and must not let your tongue be
moved by an outburst of anger, violence or temper. It is not
merely the quarrel itself which is bad in its results; it is the
fact that you lend your tongue for the projection of bad
vibrations into the atmosphere, for nothing is more contagious than the vibrations of sound and by giving these
movements the opportunity to express themselves, you
perpetuate them in you and in others.

Among the most undesirable kinds of talkativeness should
be included all that one says about others.

Unless you are responsible for certain persons as guar-
dian, teacher or departmental head, you have no concern
at all with what others do or do not do. You must refrain
from talking about them, to give your opinion upon them
and upon what they do or to repeat what others may think
or say of them.

It may be that the very nature of your occupation makes
it your duty to report what is happening in a particular de-

partment or business undertaking or a common work. In that case, the report should be confined to the work alone and not touch personal matters. It should be in every way wholly objective. You must not allow any personal reaction, preference, sympathy or antipathy to enter there. Particularly, never mix up your petty personal grudge into the work assigned to you.

In any case and as a general rule, the less one speaks of others — even if it be in praise of them — the better it is. Already it is so difficult to know exactly what happens in oneself, how to know then with certainty what is happening in others? Refrain then totally from pronouncing upon any person one of those irrevocable judgments which can only be a stupidity, if not malice.

When thought is expressed in speech, the vibration of the sound has a considerable power to put the most material substance into contact with the thought and thus give it a concrete and effective reality. That is why you must not speak ill of things or persons or speak out in words things that contradict in the world the progress of the divine realisation. It is an absolute general rule. And yet it has an exception. You must criticise nothing unless you have at the same time a conscious power and an active will in you to dissolve or transform the movements or things you criticise. In fact this conscious power and this active will possess the capacity to infuse into matter the possibility to react and refuse the bad vibration and ultimately to correct the vibration so as to prevent it from continuing to express itself on the physical plane.

This can be done without danger or risk only by him who moves in the gnostic domain and possesses in his mental faculties the light of the spirit and the force of the Truth.

He, the divine worker, is free from all preference and attachment; he has broken down in himself the limits of the ego and he is nothing else than a perfectly pure and impersonal instrument for the supramental action upon earth.

There are also all the words that are uttered to express ideas, opinions, results of reflection or study. Here we are in an intellectual domain and we might think that in this region men are more reasonable, balanced and the practice of strict austerity is less indispensable. It is nothing of the kind, however; for even here, into this home of ideas and knowledge, man has introduced violence of his convictions, sectarian intolerance, passion of preference. Here also there will be the same need to have recourse to mental austerity and to carefully avoid all exchange of ideas that leads very often to bitter and almost always inane controversy, avoid too all oppositions of opinions which end in hot discussion and even dispute, arising always from the mind's narrowness, a thing that can be cured easily when one ascends high enough in the mental domain.

Indeed, sectarianism becomes impossible when one knows that all formulated thought is only one way of saying something which escapes all expression. Every idea contains a little of the truth or an aspect of the truth. But there is no idea which is in itself absolutely true.

This sense of the relativity of things is a powerful help to maintain one's poise and preserve a serene balance in one's talk. I heard an old occultist who had some knowledge saying, "There is nothing which is essentially bad: there are only things that are not in their place. Put each thing in its proper place, and you will get a harmonious world".

Yet, from the point of view of action, the value of an idea is in proportion to its pragmatic power. This power, it is true, varies much according to the individual in whom it acts. A particular idea that has a great driving force in one individual fails totally in another. But this power itself is contagious. Certain ideas are able to transform the world. It is these that ought to be expressed; they are the guiding stars in the firmament of the spirit, it is they that will lead the earth towards her supreme realisation.

Lastly, we have all the words that are spoken for the purpose of teaching. This class extends from the kindergarten right up to the university course, not omitting all the artistic and literary creations of mankind that mean to be either entertaining or instructive. In this region all depends upon the value of the work; and the subject is too vast to be treated here. It is a fact, however, that care for education is very much in vogue nowadays and praiseworthy attempts have been made to make use of the latest scientific discoveries and place them at the service of education. But even in this matter there is need of austerity for the aspirant of the truth.

It is generally taken for granted that in the procedure of education a certain kind of light, entertaining, even frivolous creations should be admitted in order to reduce the strain of the effort, to give ease to the children, even to the adults. From a certain point of view this is true; but unfortunately this recognition has served as an excuse for importing a whole class of things which are nothing else than the flowering of all that is vulgar, crude and low in human nature. The most ignoble instincts, the most depraved taste find in this recognition a good excuse to display and impose themselves as inevitable necessities. However it is not so; one can relax oneself without being dissolute, one can be at rest without being vulgar, one can become slack without allowing any of the grosser elements in one's nature to come up. But from the point of view of austerity, these needs themselves change their nature: relaxation is transformed into an inner silence, rest into contemplation and slackening into felicity.

This need, so generally recognised, of distraction, relaxation of effort, a more or less long and total forgetfulness of life's goal, forgetfulness of the very reason of existence must not be considered quite a natural and indispensable, thing, but as a weakness to which one yields because of the lack of intensity in aspiration, the instability of will, because of ignorance, unconsciousness and listlessness. Do not justify these movements and soon you will perceive that they are not necessary and at some time they will even become to you repugnant and inadmissible. Then quite a large part of human creations, ostensibly recreative but truly degrading, will lose their support and encouragement.

However, one must not believe that the value of the spoken word depends upon the nature of the subject of conversation. One can talk away on spiritual subjects as much as on any other: but this kind of talkativeness may be among the most dangerous. The new sadhak, for example, is always eager to share with others the little he has learnt. But as he advances on the path, he finds more and more that he does not know much and that before trying to instruct others, he must be sure of the value of his knowledge, until finally he becomes wise and realises that a good many hours of silent concentration are needed to be able to speak usefully for a few minutes. Besides, in the matter of inner life and spiritual effort, the use of speech should be put under a still more stringent rule: nothing should be spoken unless it is absolutely necessary to do so.

It is a very well-known fact that one has never to speak of one's spiritual experiences, if one were not to see vanishing in a moment the energy accumulated in an experience which is meant to hasten one's progress. The only exception to the rule allowable is with regard to one's Guru, when one wants to get from him some explanation or instruction about the content and meaning of one's experience. Indeed, it is to the Guru alone that one can speak of these things without danger, for only the Guru is able, in his knowledge, to turn to your good the elements of your experience as steps towards new ascents.

It is true that the Guru himself is under the same rule of silence with regard to what concerns him personally. In Nature everything is in movement and whatever does not move forward is bound to move backward. The Guru, even like his disciple, should also progress, although his progress may not be on the same plane. To him, too, to speak of his experiences is not helpful: the dynamic force of progress contained in the experience, if it is put into words, evaporates in a large measure. On the other hand, by explaining to the disciples his experiences he powerfully helps their understanding and therefore their progress. It is for him in his wisdom to know to what extent he can and should sacrifice the one to the other. It goes without saying that no boasting or vainglory should enter into his narration; for the least vanity would make of him not a Guru but an impostor.

As for the disciple, I would tell him: "In any case, be faithful to your Guru whatever he may be; he will lead you as far as you are able to go. But if you have the good fortune to get the Divine as your Guru, then there will be no limit to your realisation."

Nevertheless, even the Divine when he incarnates upon earth is subject to the same law of progress. The instrument for his manifestation, the physical being with which he clothes himself, should be in a state of constant progress and the law governing his personal self-expression is in a way linked with the general law of earth's progress. Thus even the embodied God cannot be perfect upon earth unless and until men are ready to understand and accept perfection. It will be the day when all will be done out of love for the Divine and not, as now, out of a sense of duty towards Him. Progress will be then a joy, instead of an effort and often even a struggle. Or, more exactly, progress will be through joy in the full adhesion of the whole being and not through coercing the resistance of the ego, which means a great effort and at times even a great suffering.

To conclude I shall tell you this: if you want that your speech should express the truth and thus acquire the power of the Word, never think beforehand of what you want to say, do not decide what is good or bad to say, do not calculate what will be the effect of what you are going to say. Be silent in your mind, keep steady in the true attitude, that of constant aspiration towards the All-Wisdom, the All-Knowledge and the All-Consciousness. Then, if your aspiration is sincere, if it is not a mere cover for your ambition to do things well and to be successful, if it is pure, spontaneous and integral, then you will speak simply, you will utter the words that should be uttered, neither more nor less, and they will possess a creative power.

III

Of all the austerities this is the most difficult, the austerity of feelings and emotions, the Tapasya of love.

Indeed, it is in the field of feeling more than perhaps in any other that man has the sense of something inevitable and irresistible, a fatality dominating him which he cannot escape. Love (at least what human beings call by that name) is especially looked upon as an imperious master whose caprices one cannot evade, who strikes you as he pleases and compels you to obey him whether you like it or not. In the name of love the worst crimes have been perpetrated, the wildest follies committed.

And yet, man has invented all kinds of moral and social rules hoping to control this force of love, to make it sober and docile. These rules, however, seem to have been made only to be broken and the restraint they impose upon its free activity seems only to increase its explosive power. For it is not by rules that the movements of love can be governed. Only a greater, higher and truer power of love can master the uncontrollable impulses of love. Love can alone rule over love by illumining, transforming and enlarging it. For here also, more than anywhere else, control consists not in suppressing and abolishing, but in transmuting through a sublime alchemy. This is because, of all forces acting in the universe, love is the most powerful, the most irresistible; without love the world would fall back into the chaos of inconscience.

Consciousness is indeed the creator of the universe, but love is its saviour. A conscious experience alone can give a glimpse of what love is, its wherefore and its how. Any verbal transcription of it is necessarily a mental disguise for that which escapes all expression. Philosophers, mystics, occultists have tried but in vain. I do not pretend that I shall succeed where they failed. My purpose is to tell in the simplest terms possible what under their pen takes such an abstract and complicated form. My words will have no other aim than to lead towards the living experience and they are meant to lead even a child.

Love is, in its essence, the joy of identity; it finds its supreme expression in the bliss of union. Between the two there are all the phases of its universal manifestation.

At the beginning of this manifestation, love is, in the purity of its origin, composed of two movements, two complementary poles of the impulsion towards complete fusion. On one side, it is the supreme power of attraction and on the other the irresistible need of absolute self-giving. No other movement can do better in throwing a bridge over the abyss that was dug when in the individual being consciousness separated from its origin and became inconscience.

What was projected into space had to be brought back to itself without, however, destroying the universe so created. Therefore Love burst forth, the irresistible power of union.

It has been soaring over darkness and inconscience; it has scattered itself, pulverised itself in the bosom of unfathomed night. And from that moment began the awakening and the ascent, the slow formation of matter and its endless progression. Is it not love, under an erring and obscure form, that is associated with all the impulsions of the physical and vital nature as the push behind every movement and every grouping? This has become quite visible in the plant world. In the plant and the tree, it is the need of growth to get more light, more air, more space; in the flower it is the gift of beauty and fragrance in a loving efflorescence. And in the animal is it not there behind hunger and thirst, the need for appropriation, expansion, procreation, in brief, behind all desire, whether conscious or not? and, among the higher species, in the self-sacrificing devotion of the female for her young ones? This naturally leads us to the human species where, with the triumphant advent of mental activity this association attains its climax, for it is there conscious and deliberate. Indeed, as soon as the terrestrial development made it possible, Nature took up this sublime force of love to put it at the service of her creative activity by associating and mixing it with the movement of procreation. This association has become so close, so intimate that very few indeed have their consciousness illumined enough to be able to dissociate the two movements and experience them separately. Thus has love suffered all the degradations and thus it has been lowered to the level of the beast.

It is also from this very moment that there has clearly appeared in Nature's works her will to build up again, by stages and degrees, the primordial unity through groupings more and more complex and numerous. After having used the power of love for bringing two human beings together and creating the dual group, the origin of the family, after having broken the narrow limits of personal egoism by changing it into a dual egoism, she brought into being, with the appearance of the child, a more complex unit, the family. In course of time through manifold association between families, interchange between individuals and mixing of blood, larger groupings appeared: the clan, the tribe, the caste and the class ending in the creation of the nation. The work of group formation proceeded simultaneously in different parts of the world; it has crystallised in the formation of the different races. Even these races Nature will by degrees fuse together in her endeavour to build a material and real basis for human unity.

To the consciousness of the majority of men all this appears to be a play of chance in life: they do not observe the existence of a global plan, they take circumstances as they come, well or ill according to their own nature, some are satisfied, others dissatisfied.

Among the satisfied, there is a certain class of men who are in perfect harmony with Nature's way of being: these are the optimists. To them the day is more brilliant because night is there, colours are bright because of shadows, joy is more intense because of suffering, pain gives a greater charm to pleasure, disease bestows upon health all its value; I have even heard some saying that they are glad to have enemies, so they can all the more appreciate their friends. In any case, for all such persons, the sexual activity is a most savoury occupation, the satisfaction of the palate one of the delights of life one cannot dispense with; and it is quite natural that being born one must die: it puts an end to a journey which, if it lasted too long, would become tedious.

In short, they find life quite all right as it is and do not care to know if it has a reason or a purpose. They are not troubled by the misery of others and do not see any necessity of progress.

Such people you must never try to "convert": it would be a serious blunder. If, by mischance, they were to listen to you, they would lose their present poise without getting a new one. They are not ready for an inner life. But they are Nature's favourites; they have a very intimate alliance with her and this achievement must not be uselessly disturbed.

At a lesser degree and to a less durable extent, there are

other contented ones in the world. Their satisfaction is due to the magic contained in the action of love. Each time a being breaks the narrow limits in which he is imprisoned by his ego, as he soars up into the free air through self-giving, whether it is for the sake of another human being, or for the family or for the country or for his faith, he finds in this self-forgetfulness a foretaste of the marvellous delight of love and this gives him the impression that he has entered into contact with the Divine. But most often it is only a fugitive contact; for in the human being love is immediately mixed with the egoistic lower movements that tarnish it and take away all the power of its purity. Yet, even if it had remained pure, this contact with a divine existence could not always endure. For love is only one aspect of the Divine, an aspect that has upon earth suffered the same deformations as the rest.

Moreover, all these experiences are quite good and useful for the ordinary man who follows the normal way of Nature in her wavering march towards the unity of the future. But they cannot satisfy men who are for hastening the movement, who, in other words, aspire to follow another line of movement, more direct and more swift, an exceptional movement that will liberate them from the ordinary human nature and its endless journey, enabling them to take part in the spiritual progress which will lead them along the quickest path towards the creation of the new race, the race that will express the supramental truth upon earth. These exceptional souls must reject all love that is between human beings; for, however beautiful and pure it may be, it creates a kind of short circuit and cuts the direct connection with the Divine.

One who has known Divine Love, finds all other love obscure, mixed with smallness and egoism and darkness. It looks like a bargain or a struggle for superiority and authority: and even in the best of men, it is full of misunderstanding and sensitiveness, frictions and misgivings.

Besides, it is a well-known fact that you grow into the likeness of that which you love. If therefore you want to be like the Divine, love Him alone. One who has experienced the ecstasy of the communion of love with the Divine can alone know how insipid, dull and feeble all other love is, in comparison. And even if the most austere discipline is needed to arrive at this communion, nothing is too hard, too long, too severe, provided it takes you there; for it surpasses all expression.

It is this wonderful state that we wish to realise upon earth; it is this which will transform the world and make it a habitation worthy of the Divine Presence. Then will love, pure and true, incarnate in a body that will no longer be a disguise or a veil. Many a time the Divine sought, under the supreme form of love, to make the discipline easier and create a closer and more clearly perceptible intimacy; for this he put on a physical body similar in appearance to the human, but always, imprisoned within this gross form of matter, he could express only a caricature of himself. He will be able to manifest himself in the plenitude of his perfection only when human beings have made some indispensable progress in their consciousness and in their body. For man's vanity with its meanness and his stupid conceit take the sublime divine love, when it expresses itself in a human form, as a sign of weakness and dependence and need.

And yet man already knows, obscurely in the beginning, but more and more clearly as he progresses towards perfection that love alone can put an end to the suffering of the world; the ineffable joys of love in its essence can alone sweep away from the universe the burning pain of separation. For only in the ecstasy of the supreme union can creation find its reason of existence and its fulfilment.

No effort, therefore, is too arduous, no austerity too rigorous, if it can illumine, purify, perfect and transform the physical substance so that it may no longer conceal the Divine, when the Divine takes in it an outward form. For that marvel of love will then freely express itself in the world, the love divine which has the power of changing life into a paradise of sweet joy.

This, you may say, is the ultimate end, the crown of the effort, the final victory. But what is to be done to reach there? What is the path to follow and what are the first steps on the way?

Since we have decided to reserve love in its full splendour for our personal relation with the Divine, we shall, in our relation with others, replace it by a whole-hearted, unchanging, constant and egoless kindness and goodwill. It shall not expect any reward or gratitude or even recognition. Whatever the way others treat you, you will not allow yourself to be carried away by resentment: and in your pure unmixed love for the Divine you shall leave him the sole judge as to how he is to protect you and defend you against the non-understanding and ill-will of others.

Your joys and your pleasures you will expect from the Divine alone. In him alone you will seek and find help and support. He will comfort you in all your pain, lead you on the path, lift you up if you stumble, and if there are moments of faintness and exhaustion, he will take you in his strong arms of love and wrap you in his soothing sweetness.

Here, to avoid a possible misunderstanding, I must point

out that I am compelled, because of the demand made by the language in which I express myself, to use the masculine form when I speak of the Divine. But, in fact, the reality I speak of as love is above and beyond all gender, masculine or feminine; and when it takes a human body, it chooses the body either of a man or a woman indifferently according to the need of the work to be done.

In short, the austerity of feeling consists in rejecting all emotional attachment, of whatever kind it may be, whether for a person, for the family, for the country or any other object, and concentrating exclusively on the attachment for the Divine Reality. This concentration will culminate in the integral identification and serve as an instrument for the supramental realisation upon earth.

This takes us quite naturally to the four liberations which will be the concrete forms of the realisation. The emotional liberation will be at the same time a liberation from suffering in the integral realisation of the supramental unity.

The mental liberation or liberation from ignorance will establish in the being the mind of light or gnostic consciousness, which will express itself in the creative power of the Word.

The vital liberation or liberation from desire gives to the individual will the capacity of identifying itself perfectly and consciously with the divine will and brings constant peace and serenity as well as the resulting power.

Finally, crowning all comes the physical liberation or liberation from the law of material causation. Because you are completely master of yourself, you are no longer the slave of the laws of nature that make you act through subconscious and semi-conscious impulsions and keep you in the rut of ordinary life. Because of this liberation you can decide, with full knowledge, about the path you want to take, choose the action you want to accomplish, and free yourself from all blind determinism, allowing nothing else to intervene in your life's course than the highest Will, the truest Knowledge, the Supramental Consciousness.

AN INTERNATIONAL CENTRE OF EDUCATION*

The conditions under which men live upon earth are the result of their state of consciousness. To seek to change conditions without changing the consciousness is a vain chimera. All who have had the perception of what could be and should be done to improve the situation, in the different domains of human life, economical, political, social, financial, educational or sanitary, are precisely the individuals who have developed their consciousness more or less to an exceptional degree and put themselves in contact with higher planes of consciousness. But their ideas remained on the whole theoretical; or, if an attempt was ever made to realise them practically, it always failed lamentably in the long or short run: for no human organisation can change radically unless human consciousness itself changes. Prophets of a new humanity have followed one another, religions, spiritual or social, have been created, their beginnings were at times full of promise: but, as humanity was not transformed at heart, the old errors arising from human nature itself have reappeared gradually and after a time it was found that one was left almost at the same spot from where one had started with so much hope and enthusiasm. In this effort, however, to improve human conditions there have always been two tendencies, which although apparently contrary to each other should rather be complementary and together work out the progress. One seeks a collective reorganisation, something that would lead towards an effective unity of mankind: the other declares that all

* Reproduced with a few alterations from the *Bulletin of Physical Education*, April 1952.

progress is made first by the individual and insists that it is the individual who should be given conditions in which he can progress freely. Both are equally true and necessary, and our effort should be directed along both the lines. Collective progress and individual progress are interdependent. Before the individual can take a leap forward, it is necessary that something of an antecedent progress be achieved in the collective life. A way has therefore to be found whereby the twofold progress can go on simultaneously.

It is in answer to this pressing need that Sri Aurobindo conceived the scheme of his International Centre of Education, so that the élite of humanity may be made ready who would be able to work for the progressive unification of the race and who at the same time would be prepared to embody the new force descending upon earth to transform it. Some broad ideas would serve as the basis for organising this Centre of Education and as a guide for the programme of studies. Most of these have already been dealt with in the various writings of Sri Aurobindo and in the series of articles on Education that have appeared in this *Bulletin*.[1]

The most important one is that the unity of the human race can be achieved neither through uniformity nor through domination and subjection. A synthetic organisation of all nations, each one occupying its own place in accordance with its own genius and the role it has to play in the whole, can alone effect a comprehensive and progressive unification which may have some chance of enduring. And if the synthesis is to be a living thing, the grouping should be done around a central idea as high and wide as possible, and in which all tendencies, even the most contradictory, would find their respective places. That idea is to

[1] These are reproduced in the present book.

give man the conditions of life necessary for preparing him to manifest the new force that will create the race of tomorrow.

All urge of rivalry, all struggle for precedence and domination should disappear giving place to a will for harmonious organisation, for clear-sighted and effective collaboration.

To make this possible, children from their very early age, must be accustomed not merely to the idea but to its practice. Therefore the International Centre of Education will be international not because students from all countries will be admitted here, nor because the education will be given in their own mother tongue but particularly because the cultures of the different regions of the earth will be represented here in such a way as to be accessible to all, not merely intellectually, in ideas, theories, principles and languages, but also vitally in habits and customs, in art under all forms — painting, sculpture, music, architecture, decoration — and physically too through natural scenery, dress, games, sports, industries and food. A kind of world-exhibition has to be organised in which all the countries will be represented in a concrete and living manner; the ideal is that every nation with a very definite culture would have a pavilion representing that culture, built on a model that most displays the habits of the country: it will exhibit the nation's most representative products, natural as well as manufactured, products also that best express its intellectual and artistic genius and its spiritual tendencies. Each nation would thus find a practical and concrete interest in cultural synthesis and collaborate in the work by taking over the charge of the pavilion that represents it. A lodging house also could be attached, large or small according to the need, where students of the same nationality would be accommodated;

they will thus enjoy the very culture of their own motherland, and at the same time receive at the centre the education which will introduce them as well to other cultures existing upon earth. Thus the international education will not be simply theoretical, on the school bench, but practical in all details of existence.

A general idea of the organisation is only given here: the application in details will be shown gradually in the *Bulletin* as things are actually carried out.

The first aim then will be to help individuals to become conscious of the fundamental genius of the nation to which they belong and at the same time to put them in contact with the modes of living of other nations so that they may know and respect equally the true spirit of all the countries upon earth. For all world organisation, to be real and to be able to live, must be based upon mutual respect and understanding between nation and nation as well as between individual and individual. It is only in the collective order and organisation, in a collaboration based upon mutual goodwill that lies the possibility of man being lifted out of the painful chaos where he is now. It is with this aim and in this spirit that all human problems will be studied at the Centre of Education: and their solution will be given in the light of the Supramental Knowledge which Sri Aurobindo has revealed in his writings.

TO THE CHILDREN OF THE ASHRAM*

There is an ascending evolution in nature which goes from the stone to the plant, from the plant to the animal, from the animal to man. Because man is, for the moment, the last rung at the summit of the ascending evolution, he considers himself as the final stage in this ascension and believes there can be nothing on earth superior to him. In that he is mistaken. In his physical nature he is yet almost wholly an animal, a thinking and speaking animal, but still an animal in his material habits and instincts. Undoubtedly, nature cannot be satisfied with such an imperfect result; she endeavours to bring out a being who will be to man what man is to the animal, a being who will remain a man in its external form, and yet whose consciousness will rise far above the mental and its slavery to ignorance.

Sri Aurobindo came upon earth to teach this truth to men. He told them that man is only a transitional being living in a mental consciousness, but with the possibility of acquiring a new consciousness, the Truth-consciousness, and capable of living a life perfectly harmonious, good and beautiful, happy and fully conscious. During the whole of his life upon earth, Sri Aurobindo gave all his time to establish in himself this consciousness which he called supramental, and to help those gathered around him to realise it.

You have the immense privilege of having come quite young to the Ashram, that is to say, still plastic and capable of being moulded according to this new ideal and thus become the representatives of the new race. Here, in the

* This article was written on July 24, 1951 and included in the booklet *The Ideal Child*, 1953.

Ashram, you are in the most favourable conditions with regard to the environment, the influence, the teaching and the example, to awaken in you this supramental consciousness and to grow according to its law.

Now, all depends on your will and your sincerity. If you have the will no more to belong to ordinary humanity, no more to be merely evolved animals: if your will is to become men of the new race realising Sri Aurobindo's supramental ideal, living a new and higher life upon a new earth, you will find here all the necessary help to achieve your purpose: you will profit fully by your stay in the Ashram and eventually become living examples for the world.

WHY ARE DIPLOMAS AND CERTIFICATES NOT GIVEN TO THE STUDENTS OF THE CENTRE OF EDUCATION?*

For about a century mankind has been suffering from a disease which seems to be spreading more and more, and in our days, it has become most acute, it is what we may call "utilitarianism". Things and persons, circumstances and activities seem to be viewed and appreciated exclusively from this angle alone. Nothing has any value unless it is useful. It goes, of course, without saying that what is useful is better than what is not so. But one must first of all understand what one calls useful — useful to whom, to what, for what?

Indeed, more and more, the races which considered themselves civilised have been naming as useful that which serves to bring, to acquire or to produce money. Everything is judged from this monetary angle. That is what I call utilitarianism. And this disease is very contagious, for even children do not escape from it. At an age when one should have dreams of beauty and greatness and perfection, perhaps too sublime for ordinary common sense, but certainly higher than this dull good sense, they dream of money and worry how to earn it.

So when they think of their studies they think above all of what can be useful to them, so that later on when they grow up, they can earn a great deal of money.

And the thing that becomes most important for them is to prepare to pass examinations with success; for it is with

* Reproduced from the *Bulletin of Sri Aurobindo International Centre of Education* (Sri Aurobindo Ashram, Pondicherry), Aug. 1960.

diplomas and certificates and titles that they will be able to get good positions and earn much.

For them study has no other purpose, no other interest.

To learn in order to know, to study in order to have the knowledge of the secrets of Nature and of life, to educate oneself in order to increase one's consciousness, to discipline oneself in order to be master of oneself, to overcome one's weakness, one's incapacity and ignorance, to prepare oneself in order to progress in life towards a goal that is nobler and vaster, more generous and more true ... they hardly think of that and consider all that as mere utopia, the only important thing is to be practical, to prepare and to learn how to earn money.

Children who are affected with this disease are not in their place in the Centre of Education of the Ashram. And it is to demonstrate this to them that we do not prepare them for any official examination and competition and do not give them diplomas or titles which may serve them in the outside world.

We want to have here only those who aspire for a higher and better life, who are eager for knowledge and perfection, who look ardently towards a more wholly true future.